Baptized into Christ's Death and Resurrection

Preparing to Celebrate a Christian Funeral

Volume 2: Children

Mark G. Boyer

A Liturgical Press Book

 THE LITURGICAL PRESS
Collegeville, Minnesota

1   2   3   4   5   6   7   8   9

Library of Congress Cataloging-in-Publication Data

Boyer, Mark G.
    Baptized into Christ's death and resurrection : preparing to
  celebrate a Christian funeral / Mark G. Boyer.
       p.   cm.
    Includes index.
    Contents: v. 1. Adults — v. 2. Children.
    ISBN 0-8146-2544-4 (v. 1 : alk. paper). — ISBN 0-8146-2545-2 (v. 2 :
  alk. paper)
      1. Funeral service—Catholic Church—Liturgy.   2. Death—
  Religious aspects—Catholic Church.   I. Title.
  BX2035.6.F853B69   1999 v. 2
    264'.020985—dc21
                                  98-51062
                                      CIP

. . . God did not make death,
and he does not delight in the death of the living.
For he created all things so that they might exist;
the generative forces of the world are wholesome,
and there is no destructive poison in them

. . . .
For righteousness is immortal.

. . . [Y]ou love all things that exist,
and detest none of the things that you have made,
for you would not have made anything if you had hated it.

. . . .
You spare all things, for they are yours, O Lord, you who love
   the living.
For your immortal spirit is in all things.

—*Wis 1:13-15; 11:24, 26–12:1*

Dedicated to

Samantha Gail Pashia-McElyea,
November 30–December 28, 1995,

my first great-niece,
who in twenty-eight days of life
taught the paschal mystery
to her parents, to me, and to hundreds of friends.

Contents

Introduction

In his letter to the Romans, Paul asks, "Do you not know that all of us who have been baptized into Christ Jesus were baptized into his death?" (6:3). Then, he states, ". . . [W]e have been buried with him by baptism into death, so that, just as Christ was raised from the dead by the glory of the Father, so we too might walk in newness of life" (6:4). The point, states the apostle, is this: "If we have been united with him in a death like his, we will certainly be united with him in a resurrection like his" (6:5).

The title for this book, *Baptized into Christ's Death and Resurrection,* comes from Paul's understanding of baptism as an immersion into the death and resurrection of Jesus Christ. The subtitle, *Preparing to Celebrate a Christian Funeral,* indicates that this book serves as a guide through the *Order of Christian Funerals,* promulgated for use in the United States on November 2, 1989. This is volume 2, a guide for funerals for children. Volume 1 serves as a guide from the *Order of Christian Funerals* for adults.

This volume of reflections on funerals for children was inspired by the death of my first great-niece, Samantha Gail Pashia-McElyea, to whom this book is dedicated. Eight months into her pregnancy, my niece's doctor was concerned about the baby's weight. After tests were done, we found out that "Sammy," as she was nicknamed, was a trisomy-18 baby (Edward's Syndrome). Trisomy 18 refers to a chromosome abnormality, a genetic error, at the time of conception. For some reason, either the mother's egg or the father's sperm contributes an extra chromosome to chromosome 18. One in four to five thousand children are born with Trisomy 18.

Trisomy-18 babies have low birth weight, difficulty feeding, seizures, episodes of breathing difficulty, congenital heart disease, central nervous system problems, an increased susceptibility to infection, and other problems. Many do not live beyond the first few days or weeks. Fifty percent of them die by the age of six months, while ninety percent do not survive to their first birthday.

Sammy was born November 30, 1995; she died twenty-eight days later on December 28, 1995, in between Christmas and New Year's Day. While celebrating a simple funeral liturgy, I spoke about Sammy's birth as a gift from God which the entire family had enjoyed during the gift-giving season. Sammy had returned to the Giver, who wrapped her in a blanket of grace and bestowed upon her everlasting life.

My reflections turned to the death-aspect of the Christmas Season. True, it is a celebration of the birth of Jesus. But the day after Christmas we celebrate the martyrdom of Stephen. On December 28, we remember the death of the Holy Innocents. The next day we call to mind the memory of Thomas Becket, who was martyred in Canterbury Cathedral in 1170. The fact that the Christmas Season was a wonderful time of the year to die had become incarnate in the flesh of a twenty-eight-day-old child, who left this life and, through death, was born into eternal life.

Samantha Gail Pashia-McElyea touched the lives of more people in twenty-eight days than most of us do in twenty-eight years. Over one hundred people attended her funeral. She taught all of us the paschal mystery: the suffering, death, and resurrection that permeates all of life. Birth and death fill the Christmas Season, just like they fill our lives. Death is just as much a part of living as birth is. From her powerlessness, we learned that we can only enter the kingdom of heaven if we become like a child!

Because of Sammy's death and other deaths in my family, not to mention the many funeral liturgies which I have celebrated for people in various parishes, I have been very much involved with death throughout my life. I have read the works of Dr. Elisabeth Kübler-Ross and taught courses to high school students and adults on dying and death. Kübler-Ross's ground-breaking work got us to talk about death. Her stages of dying made us realize that the living go through the same stages after a loved one or friend has died.

Stages of Dying

In her book *On Death and Dying,* Kübler-Ross lists five stages of dying. We will review them briefly here in order to enhance our reflections and raise our awareness as we read the Scripture passages and reflections and think about the questions and journal entries in this book.

1. Denial. "No, not me," is what dying people say. This is a typical reaction when patients learn that they are terminally ill. In the

case of my great-niece, at first her parents and grandparents denied that anything was wrong with her.

2. Rage and Anger. Patients ask, "Why me?" They resent the fact that others remain healthy and alive while they are dying. God can become a target for anger, since God is perceived as imposing the sentence of death. God can take it, but it may be difficult for family and friends to cope with the rage and anger of the terminally ill person. In the case of Samantha, her parents and grandparents asked why this had happened to them, especially in light of the fact that only one out of every four to five thousand children are born with Trisomy 18.

3. Bargaining. At this stage the dying say, "Yes, me, but. . . ." They attempt to bargain with God for more time. They may bargain with others, asking them to bargain with God for more time for their loved one. The dying seem to become religious at this stage. Even those who have never prayed before seem to enter into prayer now. The bargaining process of Sammy's parents and grandparents took the form of asking for just a few more days of life for the infant, a few more days to get through the Christmas Season.

4. Depression. Kübler-Ross says that at this point the terminally ill say, "Yes, me." They mourn past losses, things not done, wrongs committed. They begin grieving and getting ready to die. As patients grow quiet, they do not want visitors. Finishing their unfinished business, such as a will, disclosing the hiding place of money, being sure that a dependent person will be cared for, is the task at hand. People are getting ready to let go. The depression entered in after Samantha's funeral. For nine months my niece and the rest of the family had been focused on the future birth of the infant. Nine months of waiting had resulted in twenty-eight days of life. All was empty and void. All members of the family had to begin letting go, not only of Sammy, but also of their future plans and dreams for her.

5. Acceptance. At this stage people are devoid of feeling. They say, "My time is very close now, and it is alright." They accept the reality of death and come to believe that it will not be their defeat, but their victory. For Sammy's parents and grandparents, this last stage took years. Everyone acknowledged her death, but it was not alright. Grieving continues as her photos are displayed and memories of her short life are recounted.

Knowing the stages of dying that Kübler-Ross has provided can help us understand what a dying loved one is going through and can aid us in helping the family member or friend in achieving the type of death wanted.

The living go through the same stages, once the loved one has died. Simply stated, the living engage in denial, refusing to believe that a loved one is dying or has died. They become angry because either the dying process or the rituals surrounding death interrupt their daily routines. They may bargain, figure out ways to avoid becoming involved in either the process of dying or the process of final disposition. Depression may set in as the realization hits family and friends that the person really is dying or has died and that they, too, will one day die. Finally, acceptance of the death arrives. And the living become more comfortable with the inevitability of their own deaths as well.

How Do We Learn to Die?

Today, we're out of sync with the natural process of death. Some people don't know how to die or how to face and deal with the death of a loved one because death is so well denied by our culture. Random violence or torture of any kind aside, we need to relearn the beauty of natural death. Because we have left our rural backgrounds and become an urban society, we no longer watch the pig being butchered or the cow being slaughtered or the chickens being killed. In a rural culture, we learned about death by watching animals die. We understood that animals die that we might live. Today, because all meat is prepared in slaughter houses, we never see the death of animals. We never feel it, smell it, taste it. Intellectually, we know that pork, beef, and chicken does not grow on a plastic plate with a cellophane wrapper, but, nevertheless, we are far removed from the reality of death. Furthermore, because few people make gardens and raise their own vegetables, we are out of tune with the way fruits and vegetables grow and give their lives to sustain ours.

Because we prefer silk flowers to real ones, which need water, trimming, and make a mess, we don't see the blossoms fade, the petals fall, and the buds drop their heads in death. Silk flowers do not die, but real ones do. We are out of touch with the reality of death when we are surrounded by silk flowers and vines.

Usually, people go away to die. When they become sick and near death, they are solemnly taken away from their home by an ambulance to a hospital, where monitors beep about life and tubes suck out one's last breath. In their older years, many people find themselves in nursing homes, waiting rooms for death. While a few relatives and friends may visit the dying in the hospital or nursing home, they never really witness it or live with it. They only visit it.

Once the dying is dead, the funeral director whisks away the body and prepares it with make-up and color and eye glasses in a fresh dress or suit. The dead look like the living. Once again, death is denied, removed. For some people, it no longer exists.

We must die from something. In the past, people simply died. If they were old, they died of old age. Now, there must be a medical reason: heart failure, lung disease, cancer. We have entered into a stage of pretend. If we can keep the heart healthy, the lungs functioning, and cancer at bay, we can live forever. That, of course, is not true. No matter how long we live, one day we will die—regardless if it is from disease or "natural causes"!

Because of our death-denying culture, it should come as no surprise that we are shocked at the death of a relative or a friend. Even if a person was elderly or had a history of heart disease or lung disease or was diagnosed with cancer and given days to live, the living are still over-powered by death's unexpectedness and their feeling of helplessness. The suddenness of death of a younger person caused by an accident, random violence, or torture adds even more helplessness to the already weighed down anchor of our death-denying society. Add to this the unexpected death of a child caused by prematurity, abuse, or disease or a stillbirth, and we have great difficulty dealing with the fact of death.

Death shocks us, rocks us from within, and grates at our thoughts because we are so far removed from it. We've forgotten or totally ignored death and the fact that dying is a part of living. Just as we grow up learning how to live, we must also grow up learning the process of natural death. Death is certain. It brings disruption and chaos to life.

Death's Initiation Rituals

When faced with death, we want to restore order to our world. And because we live in such a fast-paced society, we want the chaos to be fixed immediately. We are one person less. For the order to return, we revert to our initiation rituals, which employ the element of water. Simultaneously we send the dead to a new world where we believe they are born again and we take our leave, saying, "Good-bye."

The rituals surrounding death are similar to those encompassing birth and baptism. Before we were born, our mother's water broke. That messy event served as a herald of our imminent arrival. On the day we were baptized, water was either poured over us or we were plunged into the font and raised up in a new birth. It is no wonder that the baptismal font is called the womb of the church!

When we die, not only does water flow out of our bodies because muscles controlling bladders no longer work, but we are sprinkled with water as a reminder that we have crossed another boundary and entered into life on the other side of the grave.

After we were born and cleaned, we were wrapped in a white blanket and solemnly presented to our parents. After we were baptized, we were dressed in a white garment and told to wear it proudly and keep it unstained until we brought it to the reign of God. For our funeral liturgy, our coffin will be clothed in a white pall, a remembrance of our baptismal garment, which has been worn on our journey to God's throne.

Our first birth was from our mother's womb. Our baptismal birth was from the womb of the church. Our last birth is into eternal life. When we die, we are placed in a womb-like coffin and most likely buried in mother earth. Like a dormant seed, we await the day of resurrection.

When we were born, our birth was announced with a birth certificate and cards to family and friends. When we were baptized, the minister declared our arrival with a baptismal certificate. It should come as no surprise that our last birth, death, comes with a certificate. We will have arrived at the state of new, indescribable life.

What is old decays, dissolves, disintegrates, returns to dust. Every year on Ash Wednesday, we are reminded of that fact of life: "Remember, you are dust and to dust you will return." When we are buried, the living are told, "Ashes to ashes, dust to dust." The old must be buried in order to liberate the new. Birth into eternal life cannot happen unless it is preceded by death.

The rituals surrounding a Christian funeral are those of initiation. They give us a way of confronting the chaos of death and dealing with its reality. Like an army conquering an enemy, we surround death, kill it, and pull order and life out of it by using our rituals. The dead cross over the waters of chaos to the promised land on the other side.

What we may have failed to recognize is that we are doing this throughout our lives. We're always being re-initiated into the depths of life—of course, only after we die! In other words, every chaos we face and enter plunges us into darkness where we battle death and emerge, paradoxically, diminished but enriched. We are fuller of life and fuller of death. We have experienced being raised from the dead to new life.

Frequently, this experience occurs in relationships—friendships or marital unions. Disagreement breeds words that sting.

Both parties in the relationship have to take responsibility for the problem and the solution. This means that both die in order that both can rise to a new life as friends or husband and wife.

Employers can be so removed from their employees that they lose touch with the work their employees actually do on a daily basis. When an employee approaches the boss and offers a more efficient method for accomplishing the daily tasks, if both are willing to dialogue, enter into a mutual conversation of understanding, giving and taking, they die and rise to new life for the company.

We experience death and resurrection when making a transition from one state in life to another, such as from high school to college or from college to the work force or from single life to married life. We make choices, dying to several career possibilities in order to have one, dying to many friends of the opposite sex in order to have one in marriage. With every change there comes some death to the previous way of life. However, as one enters into the new way of life, more life begins to emerge and flow. The dynamic of death and life continue throughout our lives—until we take our last breath.

Letting go is an important part of living because it enables us to practice dying. If we've died throughout our lives, then final death will not have all the fears our culture seems to associate with it. The gospel-perspective is that of entrusting ourselves into the hands of God, like Jesus, who said that he would do his Father's will—no matter how difficult it would be or how much of it he did not know or understand.

Accepting our own mortality, which we make great efforts to cover up, enables us to live well. Living well is learning how to die well. Instead of hiding our dust with make-up and hair and beard coloring, tummy tucks and liposuction, body-building, amassing things and money to keep alive the illusion that we will conquer death, we live healthier lives by letting go. As we let go, we learn the great truth that less is more.

Technology, while it is good and can help us lead healthier lives, can lead us to believe that we will live forever. Kidney dialysis, bypass heart surgery, spare-part-organ replacement surgery, and other medical procedures mean that we can squeeze a few more years out of the old, tired body. Non-fat or low-fat foods, skim milk, no-cholesterol diets offer us more years of life. Doctors can become modern exorcists, technicians who ward off death with pills and shots, tubes and surgery. Ordinary food can become the Eucharist that sustains us in this life. And still death remains inevitable!

The lot, the end, of every human being is death. Sooner or later death comes to get us, whether we are ready or not. We can try to insure that our names will be remembered once we are dead, but that is futile. We cannot do a thing about remembrance once we are no longer here and cannot remember anyway.

Living the dynamic of death and life in the spirit is where real life is found. Dying and being reborn is the fullness of living. We can be reborn to a depth of life that we cannot imagine, let alone attempt to describe.

View of Life Influences View of Death

There are at least three images we use to think about life. Each of these influences the way we think about death. Most people think that life is linear. We enter the time-line of the world at a certain point and leave it at a certain point. Like an arrow, we travel throughout our lives until we hit the bull's eye. We're born, grow up, marry, age, die. The arrow hits the target, never to return to the archer. Pilgrims complete their journey. Throughout the years of our lives, we experience living but we are always looking back to what has been and forward to what will be. Like a river, life is flowing. We can fail to live in the present. For those who view life as a linear time-line, death is the end of our years. Like the hypochondriac in a cartoon said, "Death runs in my family."

Life can be viewed as circular. We are born, grow up, marry, age, and die. Then, someone else is born, grows up, marries, ages, and dies. And it goes on and on, like the seasons, which continue to repeat themselves: spring, summer, fall, winter, spring, summer, fall, winter. Such a circular view of living is like recycling. Every death is replaced with a new birth. In this understanding death is the end of one person's circle and the beginning of another's. Life and death just keep going on, circling.

Lastly, life can be viewed as a spiral. This is a combination of the linear and circular views. Life goes around and around, but it is going somewhere. With every experience of living, we delve deeper into the intimate dynamic of life and death and we move upward and outward into the dynamic of life and death. Simultaneously, we are enriched and diminished. In this third view, we keep growing until we discover God in the depths of our being and the universe in its limitless expanse. We discover that we are one, united with all that is in both its smallness and its greatness. Final death becomes a new experience for which we anxiously await because it will plunge us even more into the mystery of life.

Faith and Death

"It is in regard to death that [our] condition is most shrouded in doubt," states Vatican Council II's December 7, 1965, Pastoral Constitution on the Church in the Modern World (par. 18). We are "tormented not only by pain and by the gradual breaking-up of [the] body but also, and even more, by the dread of forever ceasing to be" (par. 18). However, there is "a deep instinct" within us that leads us "rightly to shrink from and to reject the utter ruin and total loss of . . . personality" (par. 18). We bear in ourselves the seed of eternity which cannot be reduced simply to matter, and so we rebel against death. We come to understand that modern technology can prolong life, "but this does not satisfy . . . heartfelt longing, one that can never be stifled, for a life to come" (par. 18).

The Pastoral Constitution on the Church in the Modern World addresses how belief in God and the faith in a life hereafter provide a sense of meaning and impose a semblance of order in a world and existence otherwise undermined by death. It says, "While the mind is at a loss before the mystery of death, the Church, taught by divine Revelation, declares that God has created [people] in view of a blessed destiny that lies beyond the limits of [this] sad state on earth. Moreover, the Christian faith teaches that bodily death . . . will be overcome when that wholeness which [was] lost [through sin] . . . will be given once again . . . by the almighty and merciful Savior" (par. 18).

God has called us and still calls us to cleave with all our being to God "in sharing for ever a life that is divine and free from all decay" (par. 18). The Constitution continues, "Christ won this victory when he rose to life, for by his death he freed [us] from death. Faith, therefore, with its solidly based teaching, provides every thoughtful [person] with an answer to [the] anxious queries about his [or her] future lot" (par. 18). We who have been made partners with Christ in the paschal mystery and who have been configured to his death can die in faith that God will raise us to new life, just like God raised Christ.

Instead of picturing death as coming to destroy us, faith enables us to picture Christ as saving us. Instead of seeing death as an end, faith helps us see death as a new beginning with more abundant life. Life is changed; it is not ended. Death is not a loss says faith, but a gain; not a parting, but a meeting; not a going away, but an arrival. Life on the other side of the grave is as much a mystery as life on this side is! We are more than we can conceive of ourselves to be! Life is a being-toward death; death is a being-toward life!

The Pastoral Constitution on the Church in the Modern World extends the offer of life after death to all people. It says, ". . . [T]his holds true not for Christians only but also for all . . . of good will in whose hearts grace is active invisibly. For since Christ died for all, and since all . . . are in fact called to one and the same destiny, which is divine, we must hold that the Holy Spirit offers to all the possibility of being made partners, in a way known to God, in the paschal mystery" (par. 22).

Who Should Use This Book?
When Should This Book Be Used?

This book is meant to be used primarily in preparation for celebrating the rites found in the *Order of Christian Funerals* at the time of the death of an infant. It can be used by members of the family to select rites and Scripture passages which best express the life of the dead child and the circumstances of death, to help meet the spiritual and psychological needs of the family and friends of the deceased to express grief and loss, to support the living as they accept the reality of death and comfort one another, and to proclaim the paschal mystery in which all share: death and resurrection.

This book can be used by those who plan the funeral rites. The last chapter provides forms upon which one can indicate Scripture passages and music which are to be used in the vigil service, funeral liturgy, committal, and Office for the Dead.

Bishops, priests, deacons, and anyone who ministers to the family and friends of the dead person at the time of a funeral will find the reflections in this book helpful, especially in conjunction with celebrating the various rites in the *Order of Christian Funerals*. The reflections form a resource which can be used for homilies or sermons and instruction based on the Word of God. The forms in the last chapter can serve as a guide in preparing the various rites and keeping a record of selections made by the family of the dead infant.

Anyone needing a guide for some thoughts about death can use this book in the fall, especially those days surrounding the annual celebration of All Souls Day, November 2. As the earth sheds her outer garments in death, we hold onto the life that will burst forth once winter has passed. The interplay of death and resurrection during fall and spring provides an opportunity to reflect on death, using this book.

Lent, that season of dust and ashes, is a good time to think about death. Not only do we recall the death of the Lord, but we think about our own. This book can serve as a guide for the reader through the Season of Lent.

Because Lent focuses on two aspects of the paschal mystery—suffering and death—and Easter on the resurrection, this book can be used as a guide throughout the Easter Season, too. Often it refers to the paschal mystery and the hope that all people share in new life beyond the grave.

Adult discussion groups and support groups for those grieving the death of an infant or a child will find this book a source for much dialogue. Members of such groups can read specific parts of the book and share their answers with each other to the questions for reflection and the journal exercises.

Since the book is a resource, there is no limit to the ways in which it can be used as a spiritual tool in preparing to celebrate the rites of the *Order of Christian Funerals.*

The Six-Part Process

The Scriptures employed in the celebration of each rite of the *Order of Christian Funerals* are the basis for this work. The six-part process stems from and is grounded in the word of God.

First, the notations for the texts from Scripture are given along with selections from Scripture for each rite of the *Order of Christian Funerals.* From the funeral rites for children selections are made from the Scripture passages in Parts I (Section 2), III (Sections 14–16), and IV (Sections 17 and 18) of the *Order of Christian Funerals,* including the psalms. This book follows the order of the rites in the *Order of Christian Funerals* for children, maintaining the section numbers of the *Order,* cross-referencing Scripture passages when they are used in more than one rite, and maintaining the language used in the *Order.*

Second, a reference from the English translation of the *Order of Christian Funerals* has been selected to complement the Scripture choice or develop a deeper understanding of it. The instructive material in the *Order* is a source for reflection, meditation, and guidance. Those desiring to read the paragraph references to the *Order* can find them in either *Order of Christian Funerals: General Introduction and Pastoral Notes: Liturgy Documentary Series 8* (Washington, D.C.: Office for Publishing and Promotion Services, United States Catholic Conference, 1989) or *Order of Christian Funerals* (Collegeville, Minn.: The Liturgical Press, 1989).

A reflection forms the third part of the process. The reflection presents ideas about how we might approach the Scripture passage and the reference from the *Order of Christian Funerals.* The reflection develops key themes, images, and words found in the Scripture selection and the provided reference.

Some of the reflections are general and, if used in preaching a homily, will have to be tailored to the specific vigil or funeral liturgy. We cannot be specific about what is on the other side of death, since we cannot know what's "over there." We believe that what God did for Jesus—raise him from the dead—God will do for us. The beginning and end of every reflection is faith in Christ's resurrection from the dead.

The fourth part, the questions for reflection, consists of questions which ask readers to think about a recent experience of their life and identify how God was present and active in their life. The questions are for thinking, although that does not exclude the possibility of recording some of one's thoughts. The point of the questions for reflection, which should take ten to fifteen minutes, is to see God's activity in the more recent, ordinary events of life and death.

The fifth part of the process is a prayer. It summarizes the ideas, themes, and images in the Scripture passage and the reference from the *Order of Christian Funerals* developed in the reflection and upon which one reflected using the questions provided. The prayers are personal. They praise God for gifts and calls in the past and petition for similar gifts and calls in the present and future.

Finally, a journal exercise is provided. This activity is meant to be written in a notebook or journal. The exercise asks readers to review some major events and experiences of life and death in their lives and to pinpoint how God has been leading and guiding them. It asks readers to journey backward and to mine the rich veins of their experiences of God.

The journal exercise flows out of the reflection and the questions for reflection. It builds on and is designed to expand the reader's personal reflections. Our future is conditioned by our past. Often we are warmed by fires we did not build and we drink from wells we did not dig. By examining those fires and wells, we raise our consciousness of God's activity in our lives in the past, no matter if we were aware of it at that time or not. This part of the exercise will take fifteen to thirty minutes.

It is the author's hope that the reader will grow in the spirituality of the paschal mystery—the death and resurrection of Jesus Christ—and grow in life through death, being continually formed into the likeness of Christ by the Holy Spirit, a likeness begun in the waters of baptism, repeated through life, and celebrated in the rites surrounding death.

PART I

Funeral Rites

Part II ["Funeral Rites for Children" of the *Order of Christian Funerals*] does not contain "Related Rites and Prayers," . . . which are brief rites for prayer with the family and friends before the funeral liturgy. The rites as they are presented in Part I are models and should be adapted by the minister to the circumstances of the funeral for a child.

—*Order of Christian Funerals,* par. 234.

Vigil and Related Rites and Prayers

Because the *Order of Christian Funerals* does not foresee that "Related Rites and Prayers" will be used frequently for funerals of infants and children, only one reflection is provided for each of the three "Related Rites and Prayers" provided as models in the *Order of Christian Funerals* for adults, Part I: Funeral Rites; Section 2: Related Rites and Prayers.

2. Related Rites and Prayers

Prayers After Death

Order of Christian Funerals: par. 101.

READING A: I AM THERE

Scripture: (Matt 18:19-20) Jesus said, ". . . [W]here two or three are gathered in my name, I am there among them" (18:20).

Order of Christian Funerals: par. 103.

Reflection: There are at least two kinds of presence. First, we can speak about the personal, tangible, bodily presence of an individual before us. Second, we can refer to the impersonal, intangible, non-bodily presence of one through a photograph, a memory, or a gift a person gave us. During the funeral rites for an infant or a child, the minister brings these two types of presence together. The minister represents the community of believers, the body of Christ, the tangible-yet-intangible presence of Jesus today.

By praying with the family following the death of an infant or a child, the minister gathers the members of the family and offers them the awareness of Christ's presence. The prayers after death provide the minister with the opportunity to learn about the circumstances of the child's death and to pray and respond to the needs of the members of the family while bringing the consoling presence of the word of God to them.

The mourners are supported by the presence of the Christian community, who visibly represent the invisible presence of Christ. Jesus Christ is present in us, as us, and for us. He dwells "in us" as a person of the Trinity. He "is us" as we form one body with him as head. He is "for us" as our mediator with God. The infant or child, loved into existence, baptized into Christ's body, the communion of saints, has gone from a tangible to an intangible presence, from our point of view. From God's point of view, the baby is with God for ever.

We need the support of the tangible, but we also need an awareness of the intangible. Death separates us from what was once material but is now immaterial. We believe in the presence of Christ through the community of believers, represented by members of the community and the minister. We also believe in the presence of the dead child, represented by photos, toys, and the body we honor for being a member of the body of Christ and disclosing the presence of Jesus to us.

Questions for Reflection: In what ways is Jesus Christ present in you, as you, and for you? Why do you think it is important for members of the body of Christ to gather with those who mourn the death of an infant or a child?

Prayer: Eternally present God, you disclose your invisible presence through the members of the body of Christ. When I gather with two or three others, I am assured that Jesus Christ is there in me, as me, and for me, even as he is in us, as us, and for us. Use me to share with those who mourn the compassion of your Son, who lives and reigns with you and the Holy Spirit, for ever and ever. Amen.

Journal: If you have attended the funeral of an infant or a child, how important was it to the family that members of the community of believers were present? If you have not attended the funeral of an infant or a child, how important do you think it is to the family that members of the Christian community be present? Explain.

Gathering in the Presence of the Body

Order of Christian Funerals: par. 110.

SCRIPTURE VERSE A: SPIRITUAL REST

See also Part III: Texts of Sacred Scripture, 14. Funerals for Baptized Children, Gospel Readings, 1. Revealed to Infants, and 15. Funerals for Children Who Died Before Baptism, Gospel Readings, 1. Revelation.

Scripture: (Matt 11:28-30) [Jesus said,] "Come to me, all you that are weary and are carrying heavy burdens, and I will give you rest" (11:28).

Order of Christian Funerals: par. 111.

Reflection: Rest can consist of a ten- to fifteen-minute break in our workday, a pause for refreshment. Rest might consist of an hour in our favorite chair with our feet propped up. Some people may define rest as seven or eight hours of sleep in bed during the night. No matter what form rest takes, we need to lay down our burdens for a while so that we can pick them up renewed in a few minutes, an hour, or tomorrow.

Those who mourn the death of an infant or a child need physical rest, which they may not get until all of the funeral rites are finished and the final disposition of the body is completed. The grief that accompanies the death of an infant or a child takes a lot of energy—both physical and spiritual—out of us. We are drained by what may seem to be the incessant demands of the moment. There are so many details to care for and so many decisions to make.

Mourners also need spiritual rest. The various times for prayer, such as when family and friends gather in the presence of the body of the deceased infant or child, can be a moment of spiritual rest. In an atmosphere of calm and recollection, the leader of prayer invites the mourners to lay down their burdens and rest in their faith and hope for eternal life. The periods of prayerful rest enable those who mourn to continue their grieving with the support and concern of the minister and the community of believers.

The opportunity for spiritual rest can also be found after the reading of the scripture verse. If it is proclaimed non-hurriedly, there is not only an opportunity for rest in between its words, but following its completion. The pause for silence after the reading offers a moment of spiritual rest. We are rejuvenated by the word of God. That word pulls us toward Jesus, who invites us to rest in him.

The dead child, no matter what burden he or she carried, now rests in Christ. The disease, genetic defect, cancer, accident, AIDS, or whatever caused the death no longer is a burden. The child enjoys spiritual rest for ever with God through the resurrection of Jesus Christ. The mourners of the deceased infant or child can share that spiritual rest through prayer, silence, and the presence of the community of believers.

Questions for Reflection: In what ways has Jesus given you spiritual rest? In what ways have you helped others, especially those mourning the death of an infant or a child, attain spiritual rest?

Prayer: God of rest, through your Son, Jesus Christ, you invite me to lay down my burdens so that you may give me rest. In this moment of prayer, calm my anxieties and help me to be recollected in your presence. Through your word, blow into me the quiet breath of the Holy Spirit and rejuvenate me in your service. I ask this through Jesus Christ, the Lord. Amen.

Journal: Besides prayer and pauses after the scripture verse, where else do you find spiritual rest? Make a list and describe the uniqueness of the spiritual rest you find there.

PSALM A

See Part III: Texts of Sacred Scripture—16. Antiphons and Psalms, 14. Out of the Depths.

PSALM B

See Part III: Texts of Sacred Scripture—16. Antiphons and Psalms, 7. God Protects the Simple.

Transfer of the Body to the Church or to the Place of Committal

Order of Christian Funerals: par. 119.

SCRIPTURE VERSE A: REVEALED

Scripture: (Col 3:3-4) When Christ who is your life is revealed, then you also will be revealed with him in glory (3:4).

Order of Christian Funerals: par. 131.

Reflection: All of us have had experiences of the revelation of God in our lives, but these differ from person to person. The sunrise or the sunset may have been the means of God's revelation. The clear, light-blue sky or the dark deep-blue of the ocean may have been the vehicle for God to reveal God's self to us. The oranges, reds, yellows, and browns of the trees in the fall, the friendship or married love of two people, the written word of a novel or the Bible, or the spoken word of a stranger may have disclosed God to us. God uses the world to reveal God's presence to us, an action which is constant from God's point of view but momentary from ours.

God's revelation at the time of the funeral for an infant or a child is usually and rightly associated ritually with the church building, itself a physical sign of God's presence. The procession

from the funeral home or the home of the dead child to the church
or to the place of committal can be a moment of revelation.

The procession reminds us of our Christian journey throughout
life to God. For some of us the journey lasts nearly a hundred years;
for others, the pilgrimage may be only several days. The child's
earthly journey is finished, and the life now hidden by death will be
revealed one day. Our faith declares that we are not obliterated by
death, but that we continue a hidden life with God. One day that
hidden life will be revealed in its fullness.

Until the full disclosure takes place, however, the community
gathers in the church and recalls God's acts of revelation to the
dead child. The child's journey began with life—no matter how
short or long—and continued with baptism—the beginning of the
Christian life. Even if one never received the Eucharist, the child
was nourished, nevertheless, through the community, the body of
Christ. The community, another vehicle of God's revelation, commends its deceased member, with whom it shared this life, to God in
the hope of sharing in Christ's glory.

We believe that the dead child is with God. When Christ, who is
life, returns one day in the future and is revealed, those who have
died will also be revealed as already sharing in eternal life. Until
that day, the signs of Christ's glory, God's revelation, must suffice.

Arriving at the grave or mausoleum, the place of committal, we
realize that life is more than what we can see physically. The grave
is a revelation of God. Our loved infant or child placed there can become a vehicle for God's revelation, reminding us of the fullness of
life for which we wait, of whatever that glory consists. For now,
death reveals life, a life to be totally unveiled when Christ returns.

Questions for Reflection: What are some of your experiences of God's
revelation in your life? Did these experiences change your life? If so,
how? If not, what comfort did they offer to you?

Prayer: God of glory, you live eternally as one with your Son, Jesus
Christ, and the Holy Spirit, the giver of life. Through the daily reve-
lations of your love, strengthen my faith in your hidden life. When
Christ who is my life is revealed, grant me a portion of the glory he
shares with you in perfect Trinity. I ask this in the name of Jesus
Christ the Lord. Amen.

Journal: During a funeral, what are the signs of God's revelation
that you have noticed? How did these signs help you profess your
faith in the resurrection of Christ?

PART II

Funeral Rites for Children

Part II of the *Order of Christian Funerals* provides rites that are used in the funerals of infants and young children, including those of early school age.

—*Order of Christian Funerals,* par. 234.

In some instances, for example, the death of an infant, the vigil and funeral liturgy may not be appropriate. Only the rite of committal and perhaps one of the forms of prayer with the family as provided in "Related Rites and Prayers" may be desirable.

—*Order of Christian Funerals,* par. 48.

7. Vigil for a Deceased Child

Order of Christian Funerals: par. 243.

FIRST READING: WHAT WE ARE

Scripture: (1 John 3:1-2) See what love the Father has given us, that we should be called children of God; and that is what we are (3:1a).

Order of Christian Funerals: par. 246.

Reflection: The word "child" is a noun usually meaning "an unborn or recently born person." Parents call one of their offspring their child. A son or a daughter is the child of his or her parents. But there is another use of the word "child," and it is much broader. According to the author of the first letter of John, God calls every human being "child." Every person is a child of God.

From a parental point of view, we can say that once our parents die, we forfeit our status as children and become adults alone in the world. Certainly, we cannot say that we did not have parents, but after their deaths they are no longer able to call us their children. However, from God's point of view, we are children for ever. Death does not cause us to forfeit our status as children of God. God's bond of love cannot be broken by death.

Children die every day. Some deaths are caused by car and bus accidents. A child not placed into a special car seat and strapped into place with a seat belt can be thrown to the floor or into the windshield and killed. We often hear about children on their way to school in a bus that is hit by a truck or a train and some die. Crib deaths, diseases, genetic defects, parental abuse, and accidental burns all contribute to the deaths of children. The children's ward in hospitals or medical facilities devoted totally to the care of sick children are not pleasant places to visit because a lot of dying children can be found in them.

The vigil for a child who has died is adapted to meet the needs of the family of the dead child and according to the circumstances of the child's death. However, God's love for God's children cannot be diminished or eliminated by death. As stated above, we do not lose our status as children of God through death. Our relationship of love is not fractured by death. On the other side of the grave God calls us "child"—not in any demeaning or childish manner—but to refer to that relationship of love which cannot be broken by death. We are children of God for ever.

Questions for Reflection: If your parents have died, reflect on your status as an adult who is no longer called a "child" by your parents. How do you feel about the loss of your status as a "child"? How are the bonds of love between you and your dead parents maintained? If your parents have not died, reflect on what you think your status as an adult, no longer called a "child" by your parents, will be like.

Prayer: God of love, death cannot break the bonds of love which you have established with all your children. On the other side of the grave you continue to call me to life in Christ, your Son, whom you raised from death to new life. Continue to fill me with the love of the Holy Spirit, who binds all people together as your children. I ask this in the name of Jesus Christ, the Lord. Amen.

Journal: In what events of your life have you experienced God's love for you? How were those experiences reflections of being a child of God?

RESPONSORIAL PSALM: GOD'S HOUSE

See also Part III: Texts of Sacred Scripture, 14. Funerals for Baptized Children, Responsorial Psalms, 1. Rod and Staff.

Scripture: (Ps 23)

The LORD is my shepherd, I shall not want.

. . . .
Surely goodness and mercy shall follow me
  all the days of my life,
and I shall dwell in the house of the LORD
  my whole life long (23:1, 6).

Order of Christian Funerals: par. 244.

Reflection: Most people live in houses. They may refer to them as apartments, tents, igloos, hermitages, cottages, caves, or other names, but generically the word "house" will cover all of them. If we stand back for a moment and see the earth from God's perspective, like the earthrise photo once taken by astronauts, we see a marbled blue and white sphere. Realizing that the globe is but one planet circling the sun, we come to understand that the earth is the house for all people since all of us live on and in it.

The words of the psalmist about living in God's house—here meaning the Temple in Jerusalem—aptly can be applied to the earth as the house for all. We live in God's house our whole lives, no matter whether in a physical structure called a house or simply on the third planet from the sun. God's house consists of all that exists.

The vigil for a dead child can be celebrated in the home, the funeral home, or the church. All three are appropriate places for prayer, depending upon the circumstances. The home can serve as a reminder of our heavenly home with God. Just as the child lived in the house, so now the child lives with God in God's house. The funeral home offers a larger space in which family and friends can gather. As a "neutral" space, it may be more inviting for some people who prefer not to impose upon a family in their home at the time of death. The church, the community's house for prayer, is appropriate because it is a sign of God's house and of how God lives in and with people.

Death makes us realize that God's house is bigger than just the earth. Indeed, the whole universe, whose vastness of galaxies with stars and solar systems we cannot begin to imagine and a photo of which is impossible, is God's house. On the other side of death, we believe that we, metaphorically speaking, go to live in God's house for ever. The vastness of God's house is not limited to our conceptions or our photographs.

Questions for Reflection: What do the words of the psalmist about dwelling in the house of God one's whole life mean to you? How do you picture the house of God? Who lives in it?

Prayer: Living God, all things have their origin in you. From the moment of conception to death you guide me with your goodness and mercy. Make me grateful for your love and lead me through death to the joy of your presence in your house, where you dwell with your Son, Jesus Christ, and the Holy Spirit, one God, for ever and ever. Amen.

Journal: What are the signs of God's presence in your house? What are the signs of God's presence in a funeral home? What are the signs of God's presence in a church? How do those signs help you realize that the whole universe is God's house?

GOSPEL: CONCERN FOR CHILDREN

See also Part III: Texts of Sacred Scripture, 14. Funerals for Baptized Children, Gospel Readings, 2. Like a Child.

Scripture: (Mark 10:13-16) [Jesus] took [the little children] up in his arms, laid his hands on them, and blessed them (10:16).

Order of Christian Funerals: par. 246.

Reflection: Some adults just seem to care for children naturally. They are able to anticipate their needs and direct them with little or no friction. In Mark's Gospel, Jesus is portrayed as one of these adults.

Jesus' concern for children is contrasted to the adult male disciples' lack of concern in Mark's Gospel. The author depicts Jesus' followers as trying to shoo away the children from Jesus. Such a portrayal is typical of the world of the first century in which children had no rights and were considered the property of their parents to be disposed of as they saw fit.

In two ways the Markan Jesus raises children to full human status with individual rights. First, he declares them as models of how we enter God's realm—powerlessly and dependently. Second, he lays his hands on them and blesses them.

Today, children have more rights than they did in the first century, but, nevertheless, they still die of natural causes, not to mention neglect and abuse. No matter what the cause of death, they remain models of how we enter into the reign of God—totally dependent upon God and blessed by Jesus.

Our concern for children is demonstrated during the vigil for a dead child. If the child was in the early years of elementary school and a large number of classmates are present, the vigil can be shortened for the benefit of the children. To help the children deal with the death of their classmate, some of the things they shared in school, such as textbooks or an art project, may be employed in the vigil with the children serving as commentators on the meaning of the objects. Children can be incorporated as ministers in the rite, serving as readers of the scripture verses and the general intercessions. The biblical texts can be taken from *The Contemporary English Version*, the translation used in the *Lectionary for Masses with Children*. More ideas as to the involvement of children in the vigil can be found in the Directory for Masses with Children.

The point of showing concern for children during the vigil for a dead child is to aide them in expressing their grief for the child who has died. Children are capable of understanding the reality of death, and they should not be protected from it. Adults must be careful not to let their perspective of God's reign block them from approaching it in the manner of a child—open, free, and blessed.

Questions for Reflection: Whom do you know as "a natural" when it comes to the care and concern for children? How do they demonstrate care and concern? How are they like the Markan Jesus?

Prayer: God of the child Jesus, you did not spare your only-begotten Son from the experiences of life and death, but made him like me in all things except sin. Help me to be like a child approaching your reign so that I might be blessed with the resurrection as was Jesus Christ, who lives and reigns with you and the Holy Spirit, for ever and ever. Amen.

Journal: Have you ever witnessed children participate in a vigil for a dead child or an adult? If so, in what ways were they involved? If not, what are the ways you would recommend? How are you like a child in your relationship with God?

Funeral Liturgy

Order of Christian Funerals: par. 264.

8. Funeral Mass

Order of Christian Funerals: par. 265.

A reflection on each of the readings is found in Part III: Texts of Sacred Scripture—14. Funerals for Baptized Children and 15. Funerals for Children who Died Before Baptism.

9. Funeral Liturgy Outside Mass

Order of Christian Funerals: par. 271.

A reflection on each of the readings is found in Part III: Texts of Sacred Scripture—14. Funerals for Baptized Children and 15. Funerals for Children who Died Before Baptism.

Rite of Committal

Order of Christian Funerals: par. 316.

10. Rite of Committal

Order of Christian Funerals: par. 317.

SCRIPTURE VERSE A: FROM THE WORLD'S BEGINNING

Scripture: (Matt 25:34) . . . [T]he king will say to those at his right hand, "Come, you that are blessed by my Father, inherit the kingdom prepared for you from the foundation of the world . . ." (25:34).

Order of Christian Funerals: par. 317.

Reflection: Most of us are probably not aware that our concept of linear time is a relatively new understanding. Primitive peoples thought of time as cyclical, repetitive, like a circle going around and around. Their perspective focused on the yearly cycle of seasons.

Coming on the scene and late in terms of the history of the world is the concept of time as linear. In this understanding, we see ourselves as going someplace or somewhere. Every moment is a new one which cannot be repeated. Time is thought of as a line drawn on a sheet of paper with no beginning and no end. It is infinite.

The author of Matthew's Gospel presents a story of the judgment of the nations as an occasion in linear time. The king, understood to be Jesus, returns and separates the sheep, those who are called blessed, from the goats, those who are accursed. The sheep are invited by the king to enter into the realm which has been prepared for them "from the foundation of the world" by God. Notice that God's realm has no beginning; "from the foundation of the world" is a metaphor for saying that it has always existed.

When we celebrate the rite of committal for a dead child on the day after the funeral liturgy, the rite can be adapted by adding a song, an extra or longer passage from Scripture, and a brief homily. The purpose of adding those elements is not to lengthen the rite, but to help the mourners deal with the absence of the child here and to focus on the entrance into life on the other side of the grave. The church marks the child's entrance into God's realm, where God has awaited the arrival since the beginning of the world.

Questions for Reflection: How do you think of time: cyclical, linear, or a combination of the two? How do you think children conceive of time: cyclical, linear, or a combination of the two? How does your conception of time affect the way you live and your relationship with God?

Prayer: God of all time, from the foundation of the world you have prepared a place for all humankind. Bring into your realm people of every nation, race, and tongue that they might praise you with your Son, Jesus Christ, and the Holy Spirit, for ever and ever.

Journal: What is your understanding of infinity? What do you think about the idea that God has awaited your arrival in God's realm "from the foundation of the world"?

SCRIPTURE VERSE B: NOTHING LOST

See also Part III: Texts of Sacred Scripture, 14. Funerals for Baptized Children, Gospel Readings, 3. All Go to God.

Scripture: (John 6:39) [Jesus said,] ". . . [T]his is the will of him who sent me, that I should lose nothing of all that he has given me, but raise it up on the last day" (6:39).

Order of Christian Funerals: par. 316.

Reflection: We lose things. We lose car keys, coins, photographs. But God loses nothing and no one. God's will, according to Jesus in John's Gospel, is that nothing be lost and that all be raised up to life on the last day. The understanding of "last day" can mean either the last day of a person's life or the last day of the world.

Such hope proclaimed by Jesus assists parents faced with the death of their child, who may be buried in a grave or a tomb, cremated, or buried at sea. Such a promise of life on the other side of death can help the parents of a deceased child cope with the death and grieve the loss. Christians stare at the place of committal and proclaim their hope in the resurrection of Christ.

We do not know of what resurrection consists. We do not know the meaning of "raised up" anymore than we know the meaning of "the last day." It is a promise that Jesus gives us from God. We believe that God raised Jesus from the dead, and we hope that what God did for Jesus God will do for us.

Our language is inadequate, our words pale, and we are left barren of description in the presence of hope for resurrected life. The loss of a child in death is contradicted by the hope that God loses no one. God wills that no one be lost.

In preparing for the committal of the body of a child, we recognize that what looks lost—life—has not been lost. Resurrected life, whatever it is, consists of being found by God on the other side of death. The hope realized by the dead child becomes our hope for the same life.

Questions for Reflection: In what ways has God found you on this side of the grave? How do those experiences of being found give you hope for being found and given new life on the other side of death?

Prayer: God of hope, you did not lose your only-begotten Son to death on the cross, but you raised him to new life. Help me to face death with hope, and enable me to share my hope with those who mourn the death of a loved one. I ask this through Jesus Christ, the Lord.

Journal: Realizing that any description of hope in the resurrection is difficult, what images do you use to speak about hope? How has your image changed as you have aged? How does your hope help you understand God's promise that no one will be lost?

SCRIPTURE VERSE C: EXPECTATION

Scripture: (Phil 3:20) . . . [O]ur citizenship is in heaven, and it is from there that we are expecting a Savior, the Lord Jesus Christ (3:20).

Order of Christian Funerals: par. 9.

Reflection: When we expect something to take place, we are as sure as it is humanly possible to be that the event will occur. We often speak of a couple expecting a child or a group of people expecting to take a trip. Every year we expect to mark our birthday in some manner. Even in our daily routines we expect some form of consistency.

Death, especially the death of a child, suddenly interrupts our expectations, unless the death was preceded by a prolonged illness or a premature birth or some other disease with no cure or a genetic defect. We just don't expect children to die, but they do.

When a child dies, the church expects its members to assist in the funeral rites. To this end, they need instruction from the leaders in the parish. The Christian meaning of death needs to be explained and reflected upon. Christians believe that death is not the end but a passageway to new life, to citizenship in heaven, according to St. Paul. Death continues a person's participation in the paschal mystery of Jesus—his death and resurrection—which was begun with baptism.

The purpose of the funeral rites is to ritualize the new birth, the new life of the dead child. When our expectations for life are interrupted by death, we need to be able to rely upon something familiar, such as a ritual, to help us cope with death and grieve our loss and proclaim our faith in the resurrection. The funeral rites employ the signs of initiation into life through baptism to help us understand that death is an initiation into eternal life. So, baptismal water is sprinkled on the coffin, which is clothed in baptism's white garment and near which stands the Easter candle, the sign of Christ's triumph over death and his resurrection.

Members of the community help the family of the deceased child by anticipating what might be needed physically, such as the preparation of a meal or the cleaning of the home. Through their presence for the various funeral rites and their prayer and song, they support the family spirituality and become a living sign of hope in the resurrection. Those who are close to the family can, by listening, be the emotional support that both adults and children need when burying the body of a deceased child.

Together, the whole Christian community joins in the expectation of the coming of the Savior, Jesus Christ, from heaven. It is an expectation which is focused on intensely every Advent. It is an expectation which characterizes the funeral rites for a dead child. Our hope is centered in the expectation that Christ will return to initiate us into heaven, where we have citizenship through his death and resurrection.

Questions for Reflection: As a member of your local Christian community, in what ways have you helped the members of a family who have lost a child? How is the expectation of Jesus' return a part of your daily life? How is it a part of your prayer? How does it give you hope for new life in heaven?

Prayer: God of heaven and earth, through the death and resurrection of your Son, you have established the paschal mystery. Death gives way to the promise of new life and citizenship in heaven. Make me aware of your presence in both death and life and instill in me an expectation for the coming of Jesus Christ, who is Lord for ever and ever. Amen.

Journal: In what ways has your Christian community supported the family of a deceased child? In what ways do you think the funeral rites help the members of your community understand the meaning of death and both live it and share it with others?

SCRIPTURE VERSE D: ONE-BODY PASSOVER

Scripture: (Rev 1:5-6) . . . Jesus Christ [is] the faithful witness, the firstborn of the dead . . . (1:5).

Order of Christian Funerals: par. 3.

Reflection: The term "firstborn" usually refers to the first child to emerge from a mother's womb. That child may be referred to by the parents as "our firstborn" or "our oldest" or "our only child." But in the Book of Revelation, Jesus Christ is referred to as the "firstborn of the dead," meaning that he is the first person to have passed through death to life. In other words, Christ is the first human being to be raised by God to new life beyond the grave.

God has promised all people that they, too, will pass through death to new life. When they do so, they further enhance their status as brothers and sisters of Jesus, "the firstborn of the dead" of many brothers and sisters.

The passover of Jesus is celebrated in every Eucharist. Usually in the words of the Eucharistic Prayer we remember Jesus' suffering, death, and resurrection. We remember that what God did for God's only-begotten Son, God will do for all God's children. Just as God was present in Jesus' suffering, death, and resurrection, we are assured that God will be present to us in our suffering, death, and resurrection. Through our sharing of the Eucharist, we experience the passing over from death to life of Christ. Our passover began in baptism, our initiation into the paschal mystery of Christ.

We don't speak about the faith of an infant or a young child during the funeral. We talk about how the parents witnessed their faith and how they shared what they believe with their child in their home. At the funerals of older children, who have reached the age of reason, we do speak of their faith and how they lived it in relationship to their age.

No matter what the age of baptized children, however, we can be sure that they shared in the eucharistic passover of Christ. Some dead children may not have "made their first communion" yet, but, nevertheless, they shared in the Eucharist. St. Augustine made that clear hundreds of years ago when he wrote about children who died. He said that by the fact of being baptized into the one body of Christ, they had become members of the body of Christ. Even though they may not have physically shared in the bread and the cup, they shared in the eucharistic passover by being members of the body.

Our union with Christ through baptism means that we are also united with each other. We are one body which is strengthened by the eucharistic food. Every time the community celebrates the Eucharist, the memorial of Christ's passover from death to life, all members of the body of Christ share the passover of Jesus from death to life. Christ shares his status as "the firstborn of the dead" with us. Dead children share it now even more fully than they shared it as members of Christ's body. We await our final passover through death to the fullness of life.

Questions for Reflection: In what ways have you died, such as to a desire, a relationship, a career? What suffering was involved? What new life emerged after you passed through death?

Prayer: Faithful God, you established the eucharistic passover through the death and resurrection of your Son, Jesus Christ. Through baptism into his body, I already share in his death and resurrection. Keep me a faithful witness to the faith I profess. Engrave in my life the image of Christ, "the firstborn of the dead," of whose body I am a member and who lives and reigns with you and the Holy Spirit, one God, for ever and ever.

Journal: Through the use of a missalette, a prayer book, or a missal, read through the Eucharistic Prayers. For each one record the words commemorating the passover of Christ from death to life. Why do you think the words are slightly different in each Eucharistic Prayer?

11. Rite of Committal with Final Commendation

Order of Christian Funerals: par. 317.

The readings in the Rite of Committal with Final Commendation for Children are the same as those in the Rite of Committal. For reflections on each reading, see Part II: Funeral Rites for Children, 10. Rite of Committal.

12. Rite of Final Commendation for an Infant

Order of Christian Funerals: par. 318.

SCRIPTURE VERSE A: HEART

Scripture: (Rom 5:5b) . . . God's love has been poured into our hearts through the Holy Spirit that has been given to us (5:5b).

Order of Christian Funerals: par. 318.

Reflection: We locate our emotions in our heart by placing our hands over our chest or looking down to where our heart is found. We speak about a broken heart, an aching heart, a crushed heart, a person who has no heart. While we know that our feelings are not found in the organ that pumps blood throughout our body, we think of them as being located there and speak of them as being there.

The strongest emotion we locate in our heart is love. On Valentine's Day, people give cards with hearts printed on them. Bumper stickers carry messages with a red heart representing the word "love." Even Jesus is portrayed in sculptures and pictures as having an extra-large, sacred heart to indicate his love for people.

God's love is given to us through the Holy Spirit, the bond of love between the Father and the Son. In classical Trinitarian theology, the infinite love of the Father and the Son reveals the Holy Spirit, who is called the fire of love. God shares the love of the Trinity with us.

It is that love which we call to mind when a child is stillborn or dies shortly after birth. The minister prays with the parents to comfort them and to commend the child, the result of the union of parental love and God's love, to God. The love that sustains us from the moment of conception, and maybe even before that, continues to give us life on the other side of the grave.

While the hearts of the parents are broken when a child is stillborn or dies shortly after birth, their love for each other, a manifestation of God's love for all of us, can help them commend their child to the God of love from whom the child came.

Questions for Reflection: In what ways has God's love for you sustained you throughout your life's journey? If you have experienced a stillborn child or the death of a child a short time after birth, how were you comforted by God's love? How did you entrust the child to God?

Prayer: God of love, you live in perfect love with your Son, the Lord Jesus Christ, and the Holy Spirit. I believe that you have always loved me and shared your love with me. Continue to give me the gift of love that I might follow faithfully in the footsteps of Jesus, who loved me to his death. Hear this prayer through Christ in the Holy Spirit. Amen.

Journal: Make a list of all the emotions you locate in your heart. For each feeling you locate in your heart identify how the emotion reveals God's love for you.

SCRIPTURE VERSE B: WHAT WE WILL BE

Scripture: (1 John 3:2) Beloved, we are God's children now; what we will be has not yet been revealed. What we do know is this; when he is revealed, we will be like him, for we will see him as he is (3:2).

Order of Christian Funerals: par. 318.

Reflection: Unconsciously, we live with a future. Our daily lives are oriented to future days and years of life. Today, we make plans for what we will do tomorrow. A newly married couple makes plans for children, finances, and a home. Corporations engage in long-range planning in order to determine where the company should be in five and ten years. We continue to live, to grow, and to plan into the infinite future, even though we know that the future is finite.

One of the difficulties in dealing with the death of stillborn children or those who die shortly after birth is that they did not have the opportunity to reach some of their potential. They had no future. The children did not experience the state of always becoming like we do, the state from which we live in the present but are oriented toward the future.

However, on the other side of death we believe that we continue to become, to grow, and to head toward a future. We do not know what we will be on the other side of the grave. All we can do is postulate that we will be like God in some way. Just as we are God's children in the present moment, so in the future beyond the grave we believe that we will continue to be God's children in some way.

When children are stillborn or die shortly after birth and we lament the fact that they had no future, we can find comfort in the fact that they are with God. The God who loves us into conception and birth will show us God's face some day. We will be able to see God as God is. Certainly, the One who created us will share with us God's eternal future.

Questions for Reflection: What are some of your future plans for tomorrow, for the rest of the week, for the month, for the year, for next year? How do you continue to grow toward the future?

Prayer: God of all time, there is no past or future with you, only the eternally present moment of your love. Thank you for making me your child now. Thank you for the past days and years you have given me. Thank you for future days and years to come. When you are revealed, grant that I may see your face. I ask this through Jesus Christ the Lord. Amen.

Journal: What do you think you will become next week, next year, in five years, beyond the grave? How do your past and present experiences give you hope now that what you will be has not yet been revealed to you?

PART III

Texts of Sacred Scripture

Part III, "Texts of Sacred Scripture," contains the Scriptural readings and psalms for the celebration of the funeral. It is divided into . . . "Funerals for Baptized Children," "Funerals for Children Who Died before Baptism," "Antiphons and Psalms."

As a general rule, all corresponding texts from sacred Scripture in the funeral rites are interchangeable.

—Order of Christian Funerals, pars. 343-344.

14. Funerals for Baptized Children

Old Testament Readings

1. TEARS

See also Part III: Texts of Sacred Scripture, 15. Funerals for Children Who Died Before Baptism, Old Testament Readings, 1. God Provides.

Scripture: (Isa 25:6a, 7-9) . . . [T]he Lord GOD will wipe away the tears from all faces . . . (25:8a).

Order of Christian Funerals: par. 238.

Reflection: Tears, the overflow of saline fluid secreted by the lacrimal glands, often characterize the mourners of a dead child. The tears of the dead child's parents can carve furrows into their cheeks, make their noses run, and color their eyes red. But while tears are usually external, sometimes they are invisible and no sobs are heard. Some mourners just keep all of their grief inside and do not express it at the time of the funeral.

The community of believers is challenged by the death of an infant or a child. Tears can be a sign of the bewilderment of the members of the community, but they can also be a sign of understanding to the parents. Parents and brothers and sisters of the deceased feel lost. The world seems to get much bigger and they get smaller. Their pain is almost too much to bear. Their broken hearts, dissipated lives, and grief at the loss of what the infant or child might have been can overwhelm them. The tears of members of the community can be their support.

One of my brothers, Jeffrey Allen, died when he was six years old and I had just finished my first year of college. Jeff's death was an experience from which my parents never ever fully recovered. His death was not totally unexpected, since he had spent most of his life in and out of hospitals with heart, kidney, and liver problems. My brother's death seemed to compound my father's Parkinson's disease. It sent my mother on a tailspin of overdosing on tranquilizers that required hospital intervention.

The announcement of Jeff's death is still vivid in my memory. I remember answering my mother's telephone call from the hospital and relaying the message to my father that Jeff had died just a few minutes before Mom called. A deafening silence fell over my father, my four brothers and sisters, and me. All of us burst into tears.

Some went to their rooms, others went outside. The future of a brother would never be realized.

Every year on his birthday, more than thirty years later, I find myself not only thinking about him, but wondering about what career he would have chosen, what type of life he would have led, whether or not he would be married. I calculate how old he would have been this year and I just wonder. And sometimes my eyes get watery.

The support of the community of believers is essential for those who mourn the loss of a child. Such mourning may take a lifetime. All that the members of the community can do is keep alive the hope that God will one day wipe away all the tears—both those outside and inside—from our faces as we share the new life promised to us on the other side of death and meet again those whom we loved on this side.

Questions for Reflection: For whom do you still mourn? Are tears a part of your mourning process? How has the community of believers supported you? How does the community of believers continue to support you?

Prayer: Compassionate God, you promise me a future beyond death where all tears will be wiped away from my face. Give me the support of the community of believers, turn my mourning into joy, and let my tears be a sign of hope in the resurrection of your Son, Jesus Christ, who lives and reigns with you and the Holy Spirit, one God, for ever and ever. Amen.

Journal: If a child or an infant has died in your family, how did the community of believers help you to face the future without the child or infant? If a child or an infant has not died in your family, what do you think the role of the community of believers should be in helping a person face the future without the deceased?

2. STEADFAST LOVE

See also Part III: Texts of Sacred Scripture, 15. Funerals for Children Who Died Before Baptism, Old Testament Readings, 2. My Portion.

Scripture: (Lam 3:22-26)

> The steadfast love of the LORD never ceases,
>   his mercies never come to an end;
> they are new every morning;
>   great is your faithfulness (3:22-23).

Order of Christian Funerals: par. 241.

Reflection: The word "steadfast" means "firmly fixed in place." To love another means to put the other first, before one's self. Thus, steadfast love is solid, never wavering, always faithful to the one who is loved. According to the author of the Hebrew Bible (Old Testament) Book of Lamentations, that is how God treats us. God loves us first and never changes.

When celebrating the funeral of an infant or a child, those who plan the rites begin with the presupposition of God's steadfast love and build on it. While the funeral rites reflect the age of infants or children, whether or not they were in school, and whether or not they had reached the age of reason, the steadfast love of God for the dead children remains constant.

The circumstances of the child's death are reflected in the planning process. It may have been sudden infant death syndrome, an accidental crib death, an accident, disease, or some form of violence that took away a young person's life. However, the planning is based on God's steadfast love, which never ceases.

God's mercy is reflected through the funeral rites to the family members and the entire Christian community. The grief of the family is met with the faithfulness of God. The unexpectedness of death is confronted with the promise of newness on the other side of the grave. Every morning is the occasion for God to renew God's steadfast love for all people.

Sometimes, parents need to hold their dead infant, to name the baby if the infant was stillborn or died immediately after birth, to kiss the baby goodbye before the casket is closed, to place the dead child's favorite toy in the coffin. These acts of mourning help family members express their grief even while they remember God's steadfast love.

Before the funeral of my first great-niece, who lived only twenty-eight days, I met with her parents and grandparents to plan it and to request that they say their goodbyes before we began the liturgy in the funeral parlor. Plenty of time was provided for the parents to touch their child, to kiss her, to pin a memorial of their love for her on her dress. The grandparents laid their hands on the child's hands and supported the parents as tears ran down their faces. Once the goodbyes were concluded and the casket was closed, the service began.

In the midst of the liturgy, God's steadfast love remains a constant. God's love never falters. God's mercies never end. God comforts us in our sorrow. Each person is put first in God's steadfast love. After Jesus' death on the cross, God demonstrated God's faithfulness through the resurrection. In the face of the death of an infant or a child, we proclaim God's great faithfulness and our hope that what God did for Jesus God does for everyone—resurrection to new life.

Questions for Reflection: How has God's steadfast love for you helped you through the death of a family member? How was God's steadfast love manifested in the funeral rites for your loved one?

Prayer: Faithful God, your love is everlasting. Every morning you renew your mercy and show kindness to your people. Give an extra portion of your love to those who mourn the death of an infant or a child. Enable me to be a sign of your steadfast love and of the hope that I have in the resurrection of Jesus Christ, who lives and reigns for ever and ever. Amen.

Journal: Recall several crises in your life. How did God's steadfast love support you through each of them? How do those experiences give you confidence that God's love never ceases?

New Testament Readings

1. NEVER DIE AGAIN

Scripture: (Rom 6:3-4, 8-9) We know that Christ, being raised from the dead, will never die again; death no longer has dominion over him (6:9).

Order of Christian Funerals: par. 266.

Reflection: We do lots of things over and over again until we can do them well. We call such repetition "practice." We practice piano, baseball, and writing. As children, we practice things in order to be good at them as adults.

As we grow old, we learn how to die metaphorically through practice. We don't "play funeral," but we die to what we want to do in order to spend time with a person we love. Parents die to ownership of a new car in order to put children through college. Anytime we are faced with a choice, we must let go of one possibility in order to have the other. In other words, we die to one option.

Infants and children also practice death metaphorically. Even though they may not be conscious of it or be able to verbalize it, not always getting what they want teaches them the act of dying. An infant quickly learns that his or her cries do not insure the immediate appearance of an adult. While playing, children learn to share their toys with their playmates, learning how not to be selfish, learning how to die to personal desires.

Final death, whether it comes for a child or for an adult, means that we do not have to die ever again. Like Christ, raised from the dead by God, we will never die again. Death will never touch us. How well we learned how to die will be seen in how well we make our final exit on this side of the grave.

Because children lack experience and an understanding of death, they may need to hear some explanation of the signs used in a funeral liturgy. Certainly, we do not deny the reality of physical death, but we also do not deny our faith in the hope of eternal life. The physical signs are meant to point to an invisible reality—resurrection.

The water used to initiate us into the life of Christ through baptism is sprinkled on us to indicate our initiation into eternal life beyond death. The new white garment of baptism becomes the white pall covering the coffin. The Easter candle, whose light was entrusted to us at baptism, is placed near the coffin as a sign that the dead child has attained risen life.

If the cross is used, it represents the defeat of final death through Christ's death and resurrection from the grave. A Bible, which may be placed on the casket, is a sign of God's promise, God's covenant with people, that no person will ever be lost. Any other Christian signs that refer to the dead infant or child should have their significance explained to children who participate in the funeral.

The signs of Jesus' death and resurrection, especially the cross and the Easter candle, become the signs of every Christian's death and resurrection. They are signs that death no longer has power over Christ or us. They are the signs of our hope for eternal life.

Questions for Reflection: What was your most recent experience of dying? To what did you die? Why did you choose that death? In other words, what choice of life did you make? What serves as a sign of that death and resurrection for you?

Prayer: God of life, through the wood of the cross your Son, Jesus Christ, brought final death to an end and opened the way to eternal life. His resurrection from the grave is your promise that I will never die again, that death has no more power over me. Surround me with signs of life. On the day I pass through final death, breathe into me the eternal life of the Holy Spirit, who lives and reigns with you and the Lord Jesus Christ, for ever and ever. Amen.

Journal: Besides the signs used in the funeral liturgy, such as water, pall, Easter candle, cross, Bible, what other signs remind you of death and life? Make a list and explain the significance of each.

2. WE BELONG

Scripture: (Rom 14:7-9) We do not live to ourselves, and we do not die to ourselves. If we live, we live to the Lord, and if we die, we die to the Lord; so then, whether we live or whether we die, we are the Lord's (14:7-8).

Order of Christian Funerals: par. 266.

Reflection: Signs of belonging surround us. A plastic card with our name and unique number on it means that we belong to a book club, an auto club, or a country club. Wearing a uniform means that we have chosen a specific career, such as a nurse, a waiter or waitress, a police officer, and belong to that group of people. Other objects, such as coins, stamps, plates, or figurines, can serve as signs that we belong to a group of collectors. We belong to various groups in order to share our interests and to find like-minded people with whom we can talk about our interests.

Likewise, Christians belong. We belong to the body of Christ. The primary sign of our belonging is water, used on the day of our baptism and found near the doors of our churches. Every time we enter the church physically we dip our hand into the water, sign ourselves with Christ's cross, and remember our baptism into the body of Christ. It is no wonder, then, that at funerals for baptized children the principle sign used is water sprinkled on the coffin.

However, another sign may also be used. Of whatever that sign consists, it must somehow "speak" about belonging to the Christian community and living a Christian life. Certainly appropriate for the funeral of a baptized infant or child would be the white baptismal garment, the candle given to the parents and godparents on the day of baptism, or a baptismal certificate. Other appropriate signs of belonging to the Christian community would include a children's Bible or an icon or other image of a patron saint which was placed in the child's room.

The signs of belonging used during the funeral remind us that no matter whether we are alive or dead, we belong to Christ. Through death we pass over, like Christ, to a new dimension of life. We remain members of his body, members of the communion of saints, belonging to his body from which nothing can separate us. And that gives us plenty to talk about with others who share our interest in eternal life.

Questions for Reflection: To what groups, either secular or religious, do you belong? What is the sign of your membership in each group?

How can you lose your membership in each group? How does the fact that you can never cease belonging to Christ give you hope?

Prayer: God of the living and the dead, through water and the Spirit you bring me to life and surround me with signs of eternal life. Draw me closer to yourself and make me grateful for belonging to the body of Christ, your Son, who lives and reigns with you and the Holy Spirit, one God, for ever and ever. Amen.

Journal: If you have participated in the funeral for an infant or a child, other than the Church's signs, what sign or signs of the Christian life were used? What did the sign or signs represent? If you have not participated in the funeral for an infant or a child, what signs do you think would be appropriate reminders of belonging to the Christian community? What does each sign represent?

3. ALIVE IN CHRIST

Scripture: (1 Cor 15:20-23) . . . [S]ince death came through a human being, the resurrection of the dead has also come through a human being; for as all die in Adam, so all will be made alive in Christ (15:21-22).

Order of Christian Funerals: par. 266.

Reflection: Signs of life surround us daily. The quiet beat of the human heart pulsing oxygen-enriched blood throughout the body, the leaves of the trees or their ever-green needles, the breath of our pet dog, or the movement of the gerbils in their cage remind us of life.

For baptized Christians, the sign of life in Christ is the white baptismal garment, the clothes in which they were dressed after dying with Christ in the watery bath and rising with him to new life. During the funeral liturgy, the white pall can cover the coffin of the dead child. The pall, a sign of eternal life, represents the baptismal garment. Just as the child was clothed in Christ through baptism, so now the child is wrapped in new life through death.

The white pall represents life with Christ which began on this side of the grave and which continues on the other side of it. We believe that there is new life after death. St. Paul says that life and death entered the world through the first human beings. Jesus, a human being, through his death and resurrection, also brought life, death, and new life. If all of us die because of the first human beings, so do all of us live because of one human being.

Because the funeral rites employ signs similar to those used in the baptismal rites, it may be appropriate to bury an infant in his or her baptismal garment. Certainly, it could be placed on the coffin or on top of the pall on the coffin, forming a double sign of life in Christ. We believe that the infant or child is alive to the fullest degree with Christ.

Questions for Reflection: What is your favorite sign of earthly life? How does it function for you? What is your favorite sign of eternal life? How does it function for you?

Prayer: Eternal God of life, daily you surround me with signs of life. The beat of the human heart, the newness of the earth, the breath of your creatures help to remind me that you are the source of life. On the day of my death, wrap me in the eternal life you share with your Son, Jesus Christ, who lives and reigns with you and the Holy Spirit, one God, for ever and ever. Amen.

Journal: Make a list of the signs of life that surround you today. For each identify how it is a sign of earthly life and eternal life.

4. CHOSEN

Scripture: (Eph 1:3-5) Blessed be the God and Father of our Lord Jesus Christ, who has blessed us in Christ with every spiritual blessing in the heavenly places, just as he chose us in Christ before the foundation of the world to be holy and blameless before him in love. He destined us for adoption as his children through Jesus Christ, according to the good pleasure of his will . . . (1:3-5).

Order of Christian Funerals: par. 240.

Reflection: While we know that death is a fact of life and as certain as sunrise and sunset every day, the death of a child is more difficult for us because we, unconsciously, associate death with old age. Those who have never experienced the death of a child in their families find it hard to console those who do. That is why family members who have experienced the death of a child are better able to sympathize with a family that is struggling to accept such a death.

One aspect of consolation that can be offered when a child dies is this: God chose the child from the beginning, from before the world was created, from when there was no time. Because there is no time with God, every human being of the past, the present, and the future is known to God, who chooses us in love. We are chosen for three special works.

First, we are chosen to be holy, which means to be like God. Since God is our origin, we desire to return to the One from whom we came. That desire, often characterized as seeing God's face, means that we are devoted to God. Holiness is wholeness, a sense of inner harmony or balance between our spiritual, physical, emotional, and psychological selves. Indeed, to be like God is to be whole, complete, a desire each person experiences from deep within.

Second, we are chosen to be blameless, a state of being without sin. When God calls us, God justifies us, removes our guilt, and makes us holy. Blamelessness is not a state we can achieve on our own. It is a blessing won for us through the death and resurrection of Jesus Christ. It is a way of life which reflects the wholeness and goodness of God.

Third, God adopts us through the work of Christ. Without God working in our lives, we are like orphans, without parents, people who belong to no one. However, God has chosen us to be God's children, to be brothers and sisters of God's Son, Jesus. That adoption, sealed in the new covenant of Jesus' blood, makes us special in God's eyes.

Those three aspects of being chosen by God are aptly applied to the death of children. Children, adopted sons and daughters of God, are blameless and holy. They were chosen from before the foundation of the world by God. While we mourn the loss of children, we should also celebrate the gifts that God gave them. Those gifts have been made perfect without the help of years of life.

Questions for Reflection: Have you ever attended the funeral of a child? If so, what did you find to be the most difficult part of the funeral? If not, what do you think would be the most difficult part?

Prayer: God of Jesus, you have blessed me in Christ with every spiritual blessing and chosen me to serve you in love. Make me holy and blameless in your sight. Renew within me the spirit of adoption that I might be your worthy son/daughter through Jesus Christ, who lives and reigns with you and the Holy Spirit, one God, for ever and ever. Amen.

Journal: Reflect on your own chosenness. How have you experienced being made holy by God? How have you experienced having your sin removed, being blameless? How have you experienced being an adopted son/daughter of God?

5. ENCOURAGEMENT

See also Part IV: Office for the Dead, 17. Morning Prayer, Reading: Asleep in Christ.

Scripture: (1 Thess 4:13-14, 18) . . . [S]ince we believe that Jesus died and rose again, even so, through Jesus, God will bring with him those who have died. . . . Therefore encourage one another with these words (4:14, 18).

Order of Christian Funerals: par. 242.

Reflection: The verb "to encourage," means "to inspire with courage or hope." When used in reference to a funeral for an infant or a child, it describes the support that the community of believers gives to the members of the family of the deceased. Specifically, we who believe that Jesus died and rose also believe that all who die in Christ live with him for ever. We offer that hope to the family of the dead infant or child. We encourage the family with our faith.

Children, especially brothers and sisters of the dead child, need to be stimulated by Christian hope. They may be helped best by other children, such as classmates, playmates, and friends, who are encouraged to participate in the funeral rites. Their exercise of liturgical roles depends on their ages and abilities. Depending upon those factors, children can be encouraged to serve as readers, altar servers, musicians, cantors, song leaders, readers of the general intercessions, gift-bearers. In fact, if the number of children participating in a funeral warrant it, the funeral liturgy should be adapted according to the Directory for Masses with Children.

While children participate in the liturgical roles of the community, there is another type of encouragement which they need. They need help in facing death. They need their faith fostered. Usually, adults have difficulty discussing their faith in the resurrection with children. However, they can share with children only what they themselves honestly believe. Explanations concerning death must be given in concrete terms that children can understand.

When they speak about death, adults should be careful not to use abstractions or metaphors that children cannot understand. Death is a reality and a part of life. Children experience death when the goldfish dies, when they see the dead squirrel, hit by a car, in the street, when their pet dog dies, when the evergreen tree in the yard turns brown and dies. To say that death is falling asleep may scare children so that they refuse to go to bed. To say that death is a going away may lead them to ask about a return. Children may be invited to view the body of a deceased infant or child to say goodbye and accept the reality and finality of death, but they should not be forced.

Our faith is the source of our encouragement. We believe that Jesus died and that God raised him from the dead. We hope that what God did for Jesus God will do for us—raise us to new life.

Adults offer children encouragement, not necessarily by what they say, but through their actions. The way adults encourage one another with faith is an example to children. The completeness of the resurrection of Christ is not available to our experience on this side of the grave, so children need to be encouraged through the words, actions, and hope of adults.

Questions for Reflection: Whom have you encouraged with faith? What did you say? What did you do? What hope did you offer?

Prayer: God, my hope, I believe that your Son, Jesus Christ, died on the cross and that you raised him to new life. I believe that you will bring all who have died to life with Christ. Keep me firm in faith and give me the encouragement of the community of believers, the body of Christ, who lives and reigns with you and the Holy Spirit, for ever and ever. Amen.

Journal: How would you explain death to a child? What metaphors would you use? How would you talk about your hope in the resurrection to a child? What metaphors would you use?

6. LAMB AS SHEPHERD

Scripture: (Rev 7:9-10, 15-17) . . . I [John] looked, and there was a great multitude that no one could count, from every nation, from all tribes and peoples and languages, standing before the throne and before the Lamb, robed in white, with palm branches in their hands. They cried out in a loud voice, saying,

"Salvation belongs to our God who is seated on the throne,
    and to the Lamb!" . . .

Then one of the elders addressed me, saying,

". . . [T]he Lamb at the center of the throne will be their
    shepherd,
    and he will guide them to springs of the water of life,
and God will wipe away every tear from their eyes"
    (7:9-10, 13a, 17).

Order of Christian Funerals: par. 239.

Reflection: The Book of Revelation is called an apocalypse, a type of literature written in signs. The apocalyptic genre flourished from 200 B.C.E. to 200 C.E. Apocalyptic literature attempts to narrate the victory celebration on the other side of the grave for those who remain faithful to God during times of experiencing chaos, such as death. When children die, their parents experience a disorder in their lives that can be aptly characterized as chaos. Thus, a selection of Scripture from the Book of Revelation is appropriate. Through its narration of signs, it helps family members understand that the child has already entered into the victory celebration on the other side of the grave.

Attending that celebration is a multitude of people. They come from every nation on earth, speaking different languages but dressed alike in white robes, signifying their baptismal status, and holding palm branches, indicating their victory over death. They acknowledge that their victory over death, salvation, comes from God, who is portrayed as a king holding court and sitting on a throne, and the Lamb, a sign of the dead and risen Christ. Earlier in the book, we find that the Lamb had been slain. The author is using the image of the passover lamb, the food eaten by the Israelites and Jews to commemorate their exodus from slavery to freedom, to refer to Christ who passed over from the slavery of death to the freedom of new life.

Jesus, the Lamb of God, has not only passed over from death to life, but he has become the shepherd for all the sheep, believers, who follow him. Like the shepherd in Psalm 23, the author of the Book of Revelation portrays Jesus as leading us to the springs of the water of life, God's grace, which not only saves us from death, but guides us throughout our lives. Bathed in grace through the waters of baptism, we drink of the Holy Spirit and are enlivened by God through death to life. In other words, we pass over from death to life, just like Jesus did.

At God's victory celebration, there are no tears. All God's people are united in joy. They are so happy that they worship God and the Lamb day and night. They praise and thank God for the gift of life that sustains us through this life, but also through death and into the life that awaits us on the other side of the grave. The chaos of the experience of death gives way to the hope of the order of eternal life.

Questions for Reflection: In what ways have you experienced the chaos of death? How did the hope of sharing in eternal life help you to bring order to your life? How was the Lamb being your shepherd?

Prayer: Almighty God, salvation belongs to you and to the Lamb, Jesus Christ. Through his death and resurrection, you have led me to the springs of the water of life which flow with your grace. Wipe away every tear from my eyes as I face the death of family members, friends, and myself. Give me confidence that the Lamb will shepherd me through death to eternal life, where he lives and reigns with you and the Holy Spirit, one God, for ever and ever. Amen.

Journal: Using contemporary images, how would you update the description of the following elements of the victory celebration on the other side of the grave: throne, Lamb, white robes, palm branches, shepherd, springs of the water of life, no more tears? For example, if we were going to rewrite the Book of Revelation today, instead of portraying God as seated on a throne (a kingly metaphor), we might choose to portray God as standing behind a podium (a teacher or speaker metaphor) or sitting at the head of a meeting table (a board-chairperson image).

7. GOD LIVES WITH US

Scripture: (Rev 21:1a, 3-5a) . . . I [John] heard a loud voice from the throne saying,

> "See, the home of God is among mortals.
> He will dwell with them as their God;
> they will be his peoples,
> and God himself will be with them;
> he will wipe every tear from their eyes.
> Death will be no more;
> mourning and crying and pain will be no more,
> for the first things have passed away" (21:3-4).

Order of Christian Funerals: par. 266.

Reflection: When we speak about one person being present to another, we imply the bodily figure of one person standing face to face before another. But there are other types of presence.

We can be present through the telephone. A firm "Hello" in greeting or a soft "You have my sympathy" in comfort convey a tone of the presence of one person to another. The written words in a letter bring the writer's presence to us in a unique way through the mail. No matter if the individual lives halfway around the globe, we sense his or her presence through the letter. And, of course, we use photographs and portraits to convey presence. We display the images of family and friends in order to remind us of them. Images, captured on film, convey the presence of those we love.

In the New Testament Book of Revelation, the visionary, who calls himself John, uses the new city of Jerusalem, descending from the heavens, as a sign of the presence of the invisible God with people on the other side of death. Later in the book, John tells us that there is no need for a temple in the new Jerusalem since God lives with people. God is present to people. Wherever God is, there is no crying, no mourning, no pain, no death since all of those are antithetical to God.

When we come face to face with the death of an infant or a child, we proclaim God's presence with us and the presence of the dead infant or child with God. While we know that God dwells with us, we need to proclaim it, to be reminded of it. The full experience of God's presence is experienced only when we are set free of crying, mourning, pain, and death and enter into the new realm of existence with God—what the Book of Revelation calls the new Jerusalem.

In the funeral rites we use the Easter candle as a visible sign of the invisible presence of Christ, the first human being to pass through death to the new Jerusalem, God's home, God's dwelling place. The Easter candle signifies Jesus, who died and was raised to new life. He lights our way to God. By placing the candle near the coffin, we declare that another member of the body of Christ, the dead infant or child, has been raised to life and led by Christ into the fullness of God's presence.

We believe that God is present to us now and that God is a God of life. The experiences of God's presence that we have on this side of the grave—like being present to another through the telephone, a letter, or a picture—support our hope of being fully in God's presence, face to face, on the other side of the grave.

Questions for Reflection: In what ways have you experienced God's presence? In other words, how does God dwell with you now? How do those experiences increase your desire to see God face to face?

Prayer: God, you choose to make yourself known to me through all that you have created. Come, make your home in me. As I gradually pass away from this life, bring me to your home in heaven where my tears will be wiped away, where crying and pain will cease, and death will be no more. Enable me to dwell in your presence with your Son, Jesus Christ, and the Holy Spirit, one God, for ever and ever. Amen.

Journal: Other than bodily, in what ways have you experienced the presence of other people? What was the vehicle for their presence (such as letters, photographs)? How do these experiences of presence help you name God's presence with you?

Responsorial Psalms

1. ROD AND STAFF

See also Part II: Funeral Rites for Children, 7. Vigil for a Deceased Child, Responsorial Psalm: God's House.

Scripture: (Ps 23)

The LORD is my shepherd, I shall not want.

. . . .

Even though I walk through the darkest valley,
    I fear no evil;
for you are with me;
        your rod and your staff—
        they comfort me (23:1, 4).

Order of Christian Funerals: par. 234.

Reflection: In Psalm 23, maybe the most frequently used psalm in the funeral rites, God is compared to a shepherd who leads the sheep and provides for their needs. The danger of losing sheep is always present, but especially when moving them through a dark valley. In order to protect the flock, the shepherd carries a rod, which can be used to strike predators. For support, the shepherd carries a staff upon which to lean while standing watch over the flock. The staff, which sometimes has a curled end, can also be used to pull away brush in which sheep can get stuck or to pull sheep away from what the shepherd determines is dangerous. Just as the sheep rely on their shepherd, sings the psalmist, so people rely upon God.

At the time of the death of an infant or a child, Psalm 23 can be used as a comfort for the family. All people, both the living and the dead, are God's people, members of the flock. Just as we are led by God throughout our lives, so are we led through death to eternal life. Even in what seems to be the darkest times of our lives, such as the death of an infant or a child, God protects us. God walks with us and leads us. We have nothing to fear.

God uses the shepherd's rod to keep evil away from us. Even death is not to be feared since Jesus Christ (called "the good shepherd" in John's Gospel) destroyed death through his dying and restored us to life through his resurrection. We can be confident that God will use God's staff to keep us from all danger. Our comfort is found in the eternal shepherd of the sheep who wants no one to be lost.

The experience of the death of infants or children affects families at the heart of their existence. The members need to grieve. They may feel dazed and numb and not want to believe that death has actually occurred. Grieving may take the form of holding the dead infant or child, naming the baby if the infant was stillborn, talking about the infant or child. Grieving can also include collecting keepsakes that help family members remember the infant or child. These may consist of such things as photographs, a birth certificate, a set of footprints, a plastic arm bracelet, a lock of hair. Such mementos become signs of the relationship between the infant or child and the family members. They can become the signs of God's comfort, substitutes for the rod and staff mentioned in the psalm. Even if some people are angry with God because of the death of the infant or child, the feeling of anger can be softened by the care of the shepherd who will not let anyone be lost.

The funeral rites for an infant or a child should be adapted to the specific circumstances of the death and the needs of the family. While expressing the comfort of the shepherd, the funeral rites offer the members of the family an opportunity to do something for the dead infant or child at a time when they may feel they can do nothing.

The darkness of the valley of death is to be walked through and not walked around. The journey through the funeral rites helps the family in its search for understanding death and growing in faith in the resurrection of Jesus. We will never be the same as we were before the infant or child died, but we will be led, comforted, and protected by the shepherd.

Questions for Reflection: In what ways have you experienced God as your shepherd? How did God take care of your needs? What darkness did you walk through? How did God comfort and protect you?

Prayer: God, my shepherd, I do not want when you lead and guide me. As I walk through the dark valleys of life, guide me with the Holy Spirit. Keep me from all fear, and use your rod and staff to keep me from all harm. Lead me to the green pastures of heaven, where you live with your Son, Jesus Christ, risen from the dead, and the Holy Spirit, for ever and ever. Amen.

Journal: What modern metaphor might be used in place of shepherd in Psalm 23? In other words, what equivalent image might convey the same attributes of God as a shepherd who leads, cares, protects, and comforts?

2. FEAR

See also Part III: Texts of Sacred Scripture, 15. Funerals for Children Who Died Before Baptism, Responsorial Psalm: Teach Me Your Ways, and 16. Antiphons and Psalms, 2. Youth.

Scripture: (Ps 25)

Who are they that fear the LORD?
He will teach them the way that they should choose.

They will abide in prosperity,
  and their children shall possess the land.
The friendship of the LORD is for those who fear him,
  and he makes his covenant known to them.
My eyes are ever toward the LORD,
  for he will pluck my feet out of the net (25:12-15).

Order of Christian Funerals: par. 241.

Reflection: Fear is a strong emotion which is usually triggered by our awareness of danger. We become anxiously concerned about our health, an automobile accident, a gun shot. When fear kicks in, we marshall all of our psychic energy and prepare to defend ourselves or to take the necessary steps to protect ourselves. This is not what is meant by the "fear of the Lord."

Those who fear the Lord possess a profound reverence and awe before God. They are not alarmed by God's presence, but become aware of their unworthiness, their smallness, and their humanness before the Holy One. Like the psalmist, they trust that God will lead them in making the right choices for their lives which will result in prosperity. The awe they have for God is like the reverence one friend shows another, like the honor one party of a marriage shows the other. It is a relationship sealed in a covenant of protective love.

When celebrating the funeral rites for an infant or a child, the Christian community not only remembers the deceased and the family, but also worships the God from whom all life comes and to whom it all returns. From the psalmist's perspective, the "fear of the Lord" leads to the worship of God and the deepening of faith.

Those who plan the funeral rites design worship services that are appropriate for the age of the child and the circumstances of death and keep in mind the grief of the family. But throughout the plans, the purpose of worshiping God must be kept in mind. The psalmist's understanding of the "fear of the Lord" is the goal of fostering our faith in the resurrection of Christ and all who die in him.

Sometimes the family's grief turns into an unhealthy, but real, fear for the dead infant or child. Parents feel like they did not do enough and fear that others are blaming them and/or they are not blaming themselves enough for the death. Young brothers and sisters of the dead child may express their fear of the darkness inside the deceased's coffin. Older brothers and sisters may talk about the fear they have because their playmate did something not so good before dying and maybe won't get to heaven. Anyone can fear what may happen to the body of the dead child after it is buried or be concerned about the soul or spirit or personality.

If well planned, the funeral rites can help the family begin to address their fears and teach them the "fear of the Lord." The fear of the Lord enables us to turn our eyes toward God and to place our trust in God's hands. The "fear of the Lord" fosters our faith. God protects us and keeps us from all fear.

Questions for Reflection: What is your understanding of the "fear of the Lord"? How does the psalmist's concept of the "fear of the Lord" help to foster your trust in God?

Prayer: Eternal God, through your word you teach me your ways and you guide my choices. Strengthen the covenant of friendship-love you have made with me. Send your Holy Spirit to inspire my worship of you and your Son, the Lord Jesus Christ, who lives and reigns with you, one God, for ever and ever. Amen.

Journal: How is God your teacher? What kind of prosperity has God given to you? Describe the state of your relationship with God. In what ways has God protected you?

3. CONFLICTING EMOTIONS

Scripture: (Ps 42)

> My soul thirsts for God,
>   for the living God.
> When shall I come and behold
>   the face of God?
>
> . . . .
> Why are you cast down, O my soul,
>   and why are you disquieted within me?
> Hope in God; for I shall again praise him,
>   my help and my God (42:2, 5).

Order of Christian Funerals: par. 235.

Reflection: Sometimes we find ourselves torn by the demand to choose one of several good actions. We may have the monetary resources to help one of many charities or we may be able to donate items of food to one of several pantries from which groceries are distributed to the poor. We know that we cannot write a check to every charity, no matter how deserving it may be, and that we are not able to give canned items to every food pantry, no matter how many people it may serve. We have to choose one.

The psalmist felt torn by having to choose from many good actions. The writer of the psalm characterized longing as a thirst for God, who would be like a cold drink of water on a hot summer's afternoon. The longing for God is contrasted with the act of having one's thirst quenched by God, being seen by God, being face to face with God. What the psalmist realizes is that longing for God and being satisfied by God are both good actions. Both lead to worship and hope, which is like that of a pregnant woman waiting for what she already has—a child. In other words, the psalmist is torn between two good choices.

Already, we are in God's presence, but we thirst for its fullness, its totality, God's face. Through death, we pass into that by which we await with hope to be engulfed, immersed into the divine presence. Feeling what the psalmist felt helps us to understand the conflicting emotions which arrive with the death of an infant or a child. We are torn between celebrating the child's arrival with God and thirsting for the child to remain with us. The funeral rites are designed to help the living begin to make the transition that the dead infant or child has already made. That is why the living and their particular needs and customs help to shape the funeral rites, for the rites are for the living.

The family members who have lost an infant or child through death find themselves torn with the conflict of holding on or letting go. The funeral rites they celebrate can make them aware of their own thirst for the living God, whose presence already comforts them in their downcast state. Their disquiet can be the best worship they can offer to God. Christian hope is not extinguished by death. It causes us to thirst even more for the living God, the source of life, until that day we pass through death to see God face to face.

Questions for Reflection: How do you characterize your thirst for God? In what ways are you torn between continuing to thirst for God and having your thirst satisfied on the other side of the grave?

Prayer: Living God, like a deer searching for the cool, flowing streams in the valleys, I thirst for you. Help me to drink deeply of the river of hope for eternal life which flows from the spring of the Holy Spirit. Guide me through death to eternal life and your reign where I will see you face to face and praise you as Father, Son, and Holy Spirit, for ever and ever. Amen.

Journal: What do you think are the conflicting emotions felt by most people during the funeral rites for an infant or a child? How can these feelings help people become aware of their insatiable thirst for God now?

4. PRAISE

Scripture: (Ps 148)

> Praise the LORD!
> Praise the LORD from the heavens;
>> praise him in the heights!
> Praise him, all his angels;
>> praise him, all his host!
>
> . . . .
>
> Kings of the earth and all peoples,
>> princes and all rulers of the earth!
> Young men and women alike,
>> old and young together!
> Let them praise the name of the LORD,
>> for his name alone is exalted;
>> his glory is above earth and heaven (148:1-2, 11-13).

Order of Christian Funerals: par. 236.

Reflection: At the time of the death of a family member or a friend, especially a child, the praise of God may not be the first thing that we think about. Praise, the expression of a favorable judgment, the glorification of God for the life of a child, is difficult. But upon careful reflection we discover that it is the most appropriate action that we can take.

We cannot know the mind of God or understand God's ways. All we can do is praise God for what God thinks and what God does. God is the author of life. Thus, we cannot say that we have a right to life in the sense of having a right to exist since we are brought to life by the power of God. When new life is conceived, our response should be praise for that life. When that life emerges from the womb, we praise God for the birth. Should the child live only a few hours or days or years or months, our response should be praise for the life that God gave.

During the funeral of a child, the Christian community, the church, commends the child to God's love. We declare that love is stronger than death. The God who loves us into conception and birth also loves us through death and into life on the other side of the grave. So, we join with the other members of the church in praising God for such love.

Praise also serves to console family members and friends of the deceased. Through the prayers and songs and presence of the members of the assembly, the minds and hearts of the mourners are lifted up to praise the name of God. Caught up in the worship of the church, young men and women, old men and women, praise the author of life, whose name is exalted above earth and heaven.

We believe that the dead infant or child joins in the chorus of praise. Through God's love, no one is lost. The dead infant or child, who has passed through death to life, joins us in praise of the deeds of God. In such a stance of worship, there are no better words than "Praise the Lord!"

Questions for Reflection: What recent experience of your life has brought you to a moment of praise of God? Was it a moment of peace, standing on the shore of the ocean, viewing a mountain summit, feeling the hot sand of the desert? Have you ever experienced praise during a funeral? How?

Prayer: Praise to you, God. You are the author of all life. You loved me into existence and sustain me throughout my life. Enable me to praise you for all your gifts, even in the midst of the death of family members and friends. Help me to praise you as I face my own death. Accept this prayer of praise through your Son, Jesus Christ, who lives and reigns with you and the Holy Spirit, one God, for ever and ever. Amen.

Journal: Compose your own psalm or litany of praise to God. What aspects of death, especially that of a child, do you wish to include?

Gospel Readings

1. REVEALED TO INFANTS

See also Part I: Funeral Rites, 2. Related Rites and Prayers, Gathering in the Presence of the Body, Scripture Verse A: Spiritual Rest, and Part III: Texts of Sacred Scripture, 15. Funerals for Children Who Died Before Baptism, Gospel Readings, 1. Revelation.

Scripture: (Matt 11:25-30) . . . Jesus said, "I thank you, Father, Lord of heaven and earth, because you have hidden these things from the wise and the intelligent and have revealed them to infants . . ." (11:25).

Order of Christian Funerals: par. 23.

Reflection: Often, children have insights which they share with adults, who are caught off guard by the wisdom of children. A child can see the simplicity of life which becomes complex in the adult world. A child can point out the obvious solution to a problem to adults who are too caught up in the moment of a crisis to notice. So, we marvel at children's understanding of life and how easily they can untangle the webs woven by adults.

In both Matthew's Gospel and Luke's Gospel (10:21-22), Jesus is portrayed as praying and thanking God for infants' wisdom in terms of God's reign. The wise and the intelligent—in Matthew's Gospel these are the leaders of the people—make faith and its expression, religion, difficult for people, but infants merely accept the revelation God offers. Even more, God favors children with revelation, with insight and knowledge of God.

In the ancient world, infants and children were powerless. They were considered the property of their parents, particularly their fathers, who, once they were born, could either accept them or reject them. Rejection meant death. Being vulnerable and totally dependent upon God is how the Matthean Jesus envisions people accepting God's reign. Those who are wise and intelligent can get in the way of God's revelation.

The wisdom of children can be found in the books they read and the stories they listen to and tell. A child's favorite story may serve to illustrate a quality that was present in the life of the dead child, especially if a large group of classmates attend the funeral rites. While nonbiblical stories are not appropriate during the Liturgy of the Word in any funeral rite, they can be used at other places, such as illustrations during the homily or during the words of remembrance before the final commendation and farewell.

God's word is our source of revelation of God's ways. But we don't want to limit God, who uses stories and people to make God's presence known. In Matthew's Gospel, Jesus says that God has revealed the secrets of God's reign to infants, who cannot speak about what they have heard, but who, nevertheless, receive God's revelation. Like children, we are instructed to be dependent and open to what God may reveal to us about death here and life in heaven.

Questions for Reflection: What words of wisdom have you heard from children? Why do you think God, according to Matthew's Gospel and Luke's Gospel, favors infants rather than adults for God's revelation?

Prayer: God of heaven and earth, I thank you for having revealed the secrets of your reign to children. Give me the wisdom and intelligence of an infant that I may share in your life. Do not hide from me the glory you share with the Lord Jesus Christ and the Holy Spirit, one God, for ever and ever. Amen.

Journal: What is your favorite children's story? What does it reveal about you? What does it reveal about your understanding of God?

2. LIKE A CHILD

See also Part II: Funeral Rites for Children, 7. Vigil for a Deceased Child, Gospel: Concern for Children.

Scripture: (Mark 10:13-16) [Jesus said to the disciples,] "Let the little children come to me; do not stop them; for it is to such as these that the kingdom of God belongs. Truly I tell you, whoever does not receive the kingdom of God as a little child will never enter it." And he took them in his arms, laid his hands on them, and blessed them (10:14b-16).

Order of Christian Funerals: par. 237.

Reflection: Because we live in a society that postulates that children have the same rights as adults, the uncomfortableness of Jesus' words in Mark's Gospel can allude us. In the ancient world, children had no rights; they were powerless. They were considered the property of their parents, who decided their fate. When they were old enough, boys would be taught a trade and girls would be given as wives.

Coming as it does in the second half of Mark's Gospel, the scene depicting the children coming to Jesus and the disciples upset with them is meant to teach Jesus' followers the way of powerlessness. Jesus' powerful male disciples try to keep the powerless children away from the proclaimer of God's reign. The Markan Jesus tells the powerful men that, not only has God prepared his realm for children, but they must receive the reign like children, powerlessly, if they ever hope to enter it. Ouch! In other words, discipleship is not a position of power but one of powerlessness.

Throughout the second half of Mark's Gospel, Jesus teaches the way of powerless discipleship. Immediately following the story about the children, Jesus tells a powerful rich man, who has kept all the commandments since his youth, to sell his property, give the money to the poor, and follow him. In other words, the man is to reduce himself to a state of powerless dependency.

Later, Jesus confronts James' and John's request for the places of honor on the right and left of Jesus with a statement about the last being first and the first being last. Those who are great are servants, not royalty reigning in glory. The Markan Jesus' teaching of the way of powerlessness reaches a crescendo with his example on the cross. He dies alone, powerless. That is the way of discipleship for the author of Mark's Gospel.

While the death of a child is difficult for the parents, the support of the members of the Christian community and the message of the gospel can comfort the mourners. The child, a sign of innocence and powerlessness, has entered into the reign of God. The child teaches the members of the Christian community that the only way to enter into God's reign is by becoming like little children. In a world in which most of us spend a lot of time trying to attain power or position, the message of the child and Jesus confronts us.

There is a difference between parents who lead and guide their children and those who exercise power over them. There is a difference between the employer who wields power over employees and one who invites them into the decision-making process. After struggling up the corporate ladder of success, looking down we may be surprised to see that those we walked over are just as human as we are. Becoming like a child does not mean that we permit others to walk all over us. However, it does imply that we seek the way of powerless love, the way of discipleship, if we are to enter God's reign.

Questions for Reflection: When have you exercised power over others? When have others exercised power over you? When have you experienced the powerlessness of the gospel?

Prayer: God of children, your Son, Jesus Christ, proclaimed that your reign belongs to those who are like little children. Remove the illusions of power from my life. Help me to walk the path of powerless discipleship, following the way of Christ, who lives with you and the Holy Spirit, one God, for ever and ever. Amen.

Journal: Reflect on these attributes of a child: innocent, helpless, dependent, powerless. What does each attribute tell you about the reign of God? What other attributes can you add? How childlike are you?

3. ALL GO TO GOD

See also Part II: Funeral Rites for Children, 10. Rite of Committal, Scripture Verse B: Nothing Lost.

Scripture: (John 6:37-40 or 6:37-39) [Jesus said,] "Everything that the Father gives me will come to me, and anyone who comes to me I will never drive away; for I have come down from heaven, not to do my own will, but the will of him who sent me" (6:37-38).

Order of Christian Funerals: par. 48.

Reflection: The words attributed to Jesus in John's Gospel are comforting. Everything goes to Jesus, who presents all to God and discards nothing. In a throw-away society, such as ours, those words console us when we are faced with the death of an infant or a child. God's will is that no one be discarded.

These words of the Johannine Jesus are part of an extensive monologue, called the bread of life discourse (6:22-59), which follows the narrative of Jesus' feeding of five thousand people with five barley loaves and two fish (6:1-15). The sum of the five barley loaves and the two fish, seven, representing fullness, leads to the eucharistic reflection on the meaning of the event in the Johannine community.

Keeping in mind that God's will is that no one be driven away but that all go to God, at the time of the death of an infant or a child, the vigil and funeral liturgy may not be appropriate. If the child was premature or stillborn, if the family is new to the area and knows few people in the community, or if the family just wants a simple service, the form of prayer is provided and adapted to the circumstances to indicate that no one is lost or discarded by the church.

When my first great-niece died after having lived only twenty-eight days, her parents and I discussed funeral arrangements. Because many of their friends were not Catholics, we decided that a funeral liturgy outside Mass in the funeral parlor with final committal at the grave would be best. The celebration of the Eucharist and the reception of Communion by only a few people would have separated the members of the family from most of those who would have attended. The best solution was the form of prayer we chose which, through the use of song and response, served to unite all present into a community.

In the hectic lives that most people live today, we come and go in cars, planes, buses, and trains, and we don't often take the time to stop and to think that all of us are on our way to God. Jesus brings us to God, who desires that no one be discarded. When we mourn the death of an infant or a child, we find comfort in Jesus' words that the infant or child has gone to God. God holds everything together and desires to raise all to new life. That's the hope to which our faith clings.

Questions for Reflection: Living in a throw-away society, in what ways do the words of Jesus about all going to God comfort you? Why do you think it may be important not to celebrate the Eucharist during a funeral?

Prayer: Eternal God, you will that nothing you have created ever be lost, but that all come to you through your Son. He did your will, and you raised him to new life. Help me to go to him and to find comfort in his words. Strengthen my faith and the hope to which it clings. I ask this in the name of Jesus Christ, the Lord. Amen.

Journal: Make a list of everything that you discard or throw away today. How do you think our throw-away culture influences our attitude toward the poor, the ill, the aged, the dying, the dead?

4. COMMUNION

Scripture: (John 6:51-58) [Jesus said,] "I am the living bread that came down from heaven. Whoever eats of this bread will live forever; and the bread that I will give for the life of the world is my flesh" (6:51).

Order of Christian Funerals: par. 48.

Reflection: Most people are in communion with a lot of other people. The family is a communion of relationships between the members. A school is a communion of learning between students and teachers. The members of a church form a communion of believers. Literally, the word "communion" means "union with" and connotes "mutual participation."

We share the communion of eternal life through the Eucharist, the living bread from heaven. But it is through the death-dealing and life-giving waters of baptism that we are immersed into the body of Christ, a communion which is enlivened by the Holy Spirit. When we eat the living bread, we enter ever more deeply into communion with the members of the body and with the head—Christ. Because Christ has been raised from the dead to eternal life, our communion is one of eternal life, begun in baptism. We share in Christ's eternal life now, a communion which is designed to give life to the whole world.

When children die who have already begun to share in the living bread from the Lord's table, we focus on all the communions they shared with us and all the communions we shared with them. Death does not remove the dead from communion or put an end to our communion with them. In fact, the dead share more intimately now in the communion of eternal life with Christ.

We refer to this union of all who have gone before us in faith, all who live now, and all who will come after us as the "communion of saints." The communion is formed from all of those who have eaten living bread through the Eucharist. But it is not simply limited to those who shared the Eucharist. Baptism, which plunges us into the communion of saints, means that we share "living bread" even if we do not approach the Lord's table. St. Augustine understood this best when he was asked about children who died before they were old enough to receive the Eucharist. The bishop of Hippo made it clear that, indeed, they had shared in the living bread because they were in communion with the whole body of Christ.

"Living bread," understood as a metaphor, can refer to a few kind words, a visit made to someone who is ill, or a get-well card or letter sent to a friend. "Living bread" can point us toward serving a few hours a week in a soup kitchen, donating a few dollars to an organization that helps the poor, or volunteering to help teachers in schools. In other words, we become "living bread" for others (as members of the body of Christ), like Christ was living bread for us. And such communion brings life to the world.

Questions for Reflection: In what ways have you been "living bread"? For each way identify what type of communion you shared with others.

Prayer: God of living bread, your Son, Jesus, came down from heaven to enable me to live forever. He gave his life for the life of the world. With your Holy Spirit guide me to those who are in need that I might be living bread for them. On the day of my death bring me into the fullness of the communion of eternal life you share with Jesus Christ and the Holy Spirit, one God, living for ever. Amen.

Journal: In what communions of people are you involved (such as family, school, church)? In what ways do you participate in each? How does each nurture life in you and in others?

5. WEEPING

Scripture: (John 11:32-38, 40) Jesus began to weep. So the Jews said, "See how he loved him [Lazarus]!" But some of them said, "Could not he who opened the eyes of the blind man have kept this man from dying?" Then Jesus, again greatly disturbed, came to the tomb (11:35-38a).

Order of Christian Funerals: par. 238.

Reflection: Weeping or crying is a sign of grief. By shedding tears, we indicate that we are mourning the death of a person we loved. Weeping indicates that a person is filled with sorrow and is expressing it, pouring it out. Sometimes, weeping turns into wailing—

tears accompanied by loud sobs and cries, especially when an infant or a child has died.

In what is one of the most human pictures of Jesus, the author of John's Gospel uniquely portrays him as weeping for his dead friend Lazarus. Earlier in the story, we are told that Martha and Mary, Lazarus' sisters, had been mourning and their friends had come to console them in their sorrow. However, it is only Jesus who openly weeps before the tomb and is "greatly disturbed." This is not the usual portrait of the in-charge-of-everything, Word-made-flesh Jesus painted by the author of John's Gospel.

Somehow this part of the story made its way into the Gospel, even though we find it incompatible with the rest of John's narratives and with a Savior who's moved to emotional display by the death of a friend. In fact, the weeping Jesus is contrasted with those who wanted to know why he didn't do something to help Lazarus before he died. After all, Jesus had restored the eyesight of a blind man. Certainly, he could have done something to stop the dying process for Lazarus.

But even the Son of God needs to shed tears and to teach us that weeping is part of grieving and healing. Weeping helps the mourners to work through their loss of the dead infant or child. In a manner of speaking, weeping helps us to manifest externally how we feel internally. By our emotional display, we touch a human dimension of ourselves and others and live our grief instead of burying it deep down inside of ourselves.

The Johannine Jesus' compassion should also be the Christian community's demonstration of consolation to the members of the family of the dead infant or child before, during, and after the funeral rites. Sometimes, once the funeral rites are concluded, those participating in the funeral just leave. Maybe a meal follows, but after the meal people go home. During the weeks, months, and years that follow the death of an infant or a child, the members of the family continue to mourn and to need the support and consolation of the community of believers. In other words, the end of the funeral rites does not necessarily signal the end of the grieving process.

I didn't realize how long the grieving process lasted and how it periodically returns, even if momentarily, until I visited the grave of my great-grandmother. As a thirteen-year-old boy who had spent a lot of time with her and grew to love her, I sat near her bed and watched her die. Standing at her grave over thirty years later, I realized that I was still grieving her death. As an unannounced tear ran down my cheek, I realized again that she left her imprint on my life. I have not yet finished mourning her loss, and maybe I never will be finished. Maybe the grieving process lasts a lifetime for some people.

The community of believers, the body of Christ, both living and dead, offers support and consolation to itself. When members console each other, especially the family at the time of the death of an infant or a child, they are Jesus coming again to the tomb of Lazarus, being greatly disturbed, and weeping. However, they may need to return periodically to the grave to continue weeping with the members of the family.

Questions for Reflection: For whom are you still grieving? How often is weeping a manifestation of your grief? How does your grieving help you give support and offer consolation to others when a friend or relative dies?

Prayer: God of the living and the dead, your incarnate Word, Jesus Christ, wept at the tomb of his friend Lazarus, even while he consoled Martha and Mary in their sorrow. Fill me with the compassion of Jesus, and give me the hope of sharing eternal life with you and him and the Holy Spirit. You are one God, living for ever and ever. Amen.

Journal: Why do you think the phrase "greatly disturbed" accurately describes the grief of the members of the family of an infant or a child who has died? For you, what does weeping manifest, and how does it help in healing? Why might grieving be a lifetime process?

6. MOTHER

See also Part III: Texts of Sacred Scripture, 15. Funerals for Children Who Died Before Baptism, Gospel Readings, 3. Humanity Redeemed.

Scripture: (John 19:25-30) . . . [S]tanding near the cross of Jesus were his mother, and his mother's sister, Mary the wife of Clopas, and Mary Magdalene. When Jesus saw his mother and the disciple whom he loved standing beside her, he said to his mother, "Woman, here is your son." Then he said to his disciple, "Here is your mother." And from that hour the disciple took her into his own home (19:25b-27).

Order of Christian Funerals: par. 8.

Reflection: In John's Gospel, Jesus' mother is never given a name. She makes only two appearances in the narrative—at the wedding at Cana and at the cross, and these are connected by signs. One of the signs used is the author's reference to her as "the mother of Jesus." She is not named because "the mother of Jesus" serves not only as a sign of Mary, the woman who gave birth to him, but as a sign of the Church, which is a mother of all those who believe in Jesus. In both instances of her appearance in John's Gospel, Jesus addresses her as "woman," which serves to connect the two stories and to further indicate that she represents the Church.

The unnamed disciple whom Jesus loved functions as a sign of authentic believers. He is entrusted by Jesus into the Church's care. Likewise, our mother, the Church, is entrusted to the care of all believers. There is a dialectic established: just as the Church is mother to those who believe in Jesus, those who believe in Jesus form a collective mother who cares for each. The Beloved Disciple takes the woman into his own home—not his house. He takes her into his heart, where he offers authentic care.

The tender scene at the foot of the cross echoes the wedding at Cana story, the first of the seven major signs of John's Gospel. The wedding story, which never mentions the bride, contains the incomplete sign of the six stone water jars in which is discovered the finest wine. The astute reader awaits the seventh jar, the sign of completeness.

Not only did he provide for the wedding feast, but, through his death and resurrection, Jesus became the groom for his bride, the Church. The seventh jar finally appears. Ironically, it is "full of sour wine" (19:29) which the soldiers soak up in a sponge, put on a spear, and hold to Jesus' dying lips. "When Jesus had received the wine, he said, 'It is finished.' Then he bowed his head and gave up his spirit" (19:30). The sour wine of death becomes the best wine of the wedding feast. Jesus' work is completed; he has given birth to the church.

Standing at the foot of the cross is a trinity of women: the mother of Jesus, Mary the wife of Clopas, and Mary Magdalene. Knowing from the other Gospels that Jesus' mother is named Mary, we can say that there is a trinity of Marys at the cross. They are ministering to each other, comforting each other as mourners. They represent the feminine dimension of care that needs to be shown to the dying.

Using a Pauline metaphor, we can say that in these scenes the author of John's Gospel portrays Jesus as establishing the body of Christ, the Church. It becomes incarnate in those three women and the Beloved Disciple standing at the foot of the cross. Caring for the dying, praying for each other and the dead, supporting each other in their grief, they are a sign of what the funeral rites do—make incarnate the body of Christ out of a particular gathering of people at the time of the death of a loved one.

The whole Church is represented by the gathering of a few. But those few, who serve as a sign of the church, are mother and disciple simultaneously mourning the dead and rejoicing that the dead has entered into the eternal wedding feast in heaven.

Questions for Reflection: What do you think are other meanings for the following signs: three Marys individually and collectively, the disciple Jesus loved, "woman," "mother," "home"? How do you think those signs are connected to the wedding feast at Cana (John 2:1-12)?

Prayer: God of the cross, your Son finished the work you gave him by giving birth to the Church from his side and entrusting it to the care of those who believed in him. As I continue his mission today, enable me to care for the dying, to pray for the dead, and to comfort mourners with a mother's love. Guide me to the wedding feast where the wine never runs out and where you live and reign with Jesus Christ and the Holy Spirit for ever and ever. Amen.

Journal: Why do you think it is so important for the Church to become incarnate again and again when a member dies? How does the presence of the members of the church at the funeral rites resemble the scene at the foot of the cross in John's Gospel?

15. Funerals for Children Who Died Before Baptism

Old Testament Readings

1. GOD PROVIDES

See also Part III: Texts of Sacred Scripture, 14. Funerals for Baptized Children, Old Testament Readings, 1. Tears.

Scripture: (Isa 25:6a, 7-8b)

> On this mountain the LORD of hosts will make for all peoples
>   a feast of rich food, a feast of well-aged wines . . . (25:6a).

Order of Christian Funerals: par. 12.

Reflection: In a consumer culture where most people have money to buy whatever they need and want, we may find it hard to hear what the prophet Isaiah says. He reminds us that God provides everything for us. We have nothing that we have merited. All is a gift from God.

God's providence is described in lavish symbolic language by Isaiah. The metaphor employed is a banquet at which rich food and well-aged wines are served to the guests. The meal, served on the mountain where God lives, represents the fulfillment of people's hunger for God. In the language of Jesus, the meal is a sign of God's reign.

Today, rich food is served primarily at three major festivals: Thanksgiving, Christmas, and Easter. The turkey and dressing, candied yams, green-bean casserole, giblet gravy, cranberry sauce, and pumpkin pie form the rich foods of Thanksgiving Day. For Christmas, the table is spread with a whole ham decorated with pineapple slices and cloves, mashed potatoes, peas, applesauce, and cherry pie. The leg of lamb with mint jelly, the broccoli-and-rice casserole, the tossed green salad, and the apple pie are staples for many Easter dinners.

Today's well-aged, dry, red wines come from the Bordeaux and Burgundy regions of France as well as from the Napa and Sonoma valleys of California. The sweet, straw-colored white wines are imported from the Rhine region of Germany as well as the Mosel, Saar, and Ruhr. A good harvest of grapes produces a fine white Kabinett, which is stored in a blue bottle, pleasing to the eye and the palate.

Such rich foods and well-aged wines may not seem particularly appropriate when celebrating a funeral of a child who died before baptism. But the point of the reading—God provides—is comforting. Not meant to denigrate the importance of baptism, but equally also not to cast judgment on a child not baptized, Isaiah reminds us that God provides. Using the metaphor of meal, the prophet indicates that God provides life—now and beyond the grave.

Those non-Catholics or non-practicing Catholics, as well as all others, who attend the funeral rites can be reminded of how well God provides for all of our needs, even those of which we may not be aware. The source of all is God. Certainly, the God who gives life lavishly in this life will supply it even more in the next life which Jesus called God's reign.

Questions for Reflection: What are the signs of God's providence in your life? In other words, in what ways does God provide for you? How can your personal experience of God's providence help you at the time of a funeral of a child who died before baptism?

Prayer: God of the feast, you never cease to provide for all that you have created. Make me aware and thankful for your many gifts and inspire me to share them with others. Guide me to the eternal feast where you live and reign with your Son, the Lord Jesus Christ, and the Holy Spirit, one God, for ever and ever. Amen.

Journal: If the prophet Isaiah were writing today, what metaphors do you think he would employ to indicate God's presence (mountain) and God's providence (feast of rich food and well-aged wines)?

2. MY PORTION

See also part III: Texts of Sacred Scripture, 14. Funerals for Baptized Children, Old Testament Readings, 2. Steadfast Love.

Scripture: (Lam 3:22-26)

> "The LORD is my portion," says my soul,
>   "therefore I will hope in him."
> The LORD is good to those who wait for him,
>   to the soul that seeks him (3:24-25).

Order of Christian Funerals: par. 237.

Reflection: If we had siblings when we were growing up, most likely we said to each other, "Give me my share of the candy, the money, the room." We wanted what we thought we deserved. We wanted our part of whatever the whole consisted.

When children die before there is the opportunity to baptize them, as in a still birth or a live birth with genetic complications resulting in immediate death, Christian funeral rites may be celebrated for them, especially if their parents intended to have them baptized. The intent of the parents is enough to assure us that what could not be done by sign (pouring water) and words (I baptize you in the name of the Father, and of the Son, and of the Holy Spirit), God supplied and enabled the child to share eternal life.

The focus is not on lessening the importance of baptism, being plunged into the paschal mystery, but on the various means of baptism. Besides baptism in water, the Church believes there is baptism in blood, the martyrdom of one who professes faith but has not been baptized in water. There is the baptism of desire. A person who wants to be baptized or who is preparing for baptism (such as a catechumen) is indeed baptized. And, there is the baptism of desire that parents have for their children. If children die before they can be baptized, the Church declares that the intention of the parents was sufficient. What was intended was, in fact, done.

In all of those scenarios, God is our portion. God supplies what we cannot offer. Sometimes we think that we enact the sacrament of baptism. We pour the water and say the words. But, in reality, God enacts the sacrament. Only God knows whether we intended baptism for ourselves or our children, no matter if water was poured and words were said. We hope, like children, waiting for God to act. What God does in the lives of people—children and adults—we have no authority to judge. What we see may or may not be what God sees. God offers a share in eternal life as God wills. All we can do is accept what God offers to us and wait for more in hope. We have no claim on a share.

Questions for Reflection: Have you ever attended the funeral of a child who died before baptism? If so, what portion of eternal life do you think God shared with the child and the parents? How was that celebrated in the funeral rites? If you have not attended the funeral of a child who died before baptism, how do you understand the importance of intention on the part of the individual when it comes to celebrating sacraments?

Prayer: God, my portion, you offer me the hope of sharing life with you for ever. Give me the patience to wait for you to act. Give me the gift of a pure intention in seeking you and following your Son, Jesus Christ, who lives and reigns with you and the Holy Spirit, one God, for ever and ever. Amen.

Journal: In what ways do you think you have witnessed God's graciousness at work in your life? In what ways do you think you have witnessed God's graciousness at work in the lives of two or three other people? In what ways can you state that none of it was deserved?

Responsorial Psalm

TEACH ME YOUR WAYS

See also Part III: Texts of Sacred Scripture, 14. Funerals for Baptized Children, Responsorial Psalms, 2. Fear, and 16. Antiphons and Psalms, 2. Youth.

Scripture: (Ps 25)

Make me know your ways, O LORD;
   teach me your paths.
Lead me in your truth, and teach me,
   for you are the God of my salvation;
   for you I wait all day long (25:4-5).

Order of Christian Funerals: par. 21.

Reflection: The psalmist sings about waiting. The waiting done by the writer of the psalm is not standing in a check-out line in a grocery store, not before an ATM for cash, and not in a holding area of an airport gate before boarding the plane. The psalmist waits for the God of salvation, the One who helps us know God's ways, who teaches us God's paths, who leads us in truth. And waiting for those instructions will require a long time.

The psalmist also sings about being taught by God. That image may immediately conjure up a picture of a classroom with a teacher at the front and students sitting behind desks all placed in neat rows. That's not God's way of teaching us. God doesn't hold religion classes. God uses our senses to teach us God's ways.

The occasion of the funeral of a child who died before baptism puts the members of the Christian community in the same position as the psalmist. We wait to be taught about life—what God wants of us now—and on the other side of the grave. We want to know of what eternal life consists and what it is like. But the psalmist calls us to look deep into ourselves and, putting our trust in God, wait for God to teach us. The psalm makes us aware of our vulnerability in the presence of God and our dependency upon God's actions.

The environment in which the funeral of a child who died before baptism is celebrated can help to evoke and convey the trust in God sung about by the psalmist. God can teach us through the environment in which a funeral takes place.

Because liturgy involves the whole person, the Scriptures need to be read clearly with conviction and understanding to engage the auditory sense. The prayers need to be said with conviction overlaid with trust that God saves. Reverence needs to permeate the singing of psalms and songs. As we hear biblical passages, prayers, psalms, and songs, God teaches us.

Our sense of touch is employed through ritual gestures which help us to reflect on our dependence upon God. We join in several processions with the body of the deceased child, we stand and kneel to pray, we sit to listen. God uses our ritual gestures as vehicles of revelation to teach us trust.

The sweet-smelling incense which honors the body of the dead child not only prompts us to raise our eyes upward in prayer, but it also engages our olfactory sense. If the Eucharist is celebrated, the bread and wine of the body and blood of Christ enable us to taste of God's ways. Through smoke and food, God teaches us God's ways.

Simplicity is the key to being taught by God. God instructs us through the senses God has given us. Less is always more and encourages the active participation of all. Simplicity invites people to explore the less, to wait, and to be taught about God's way of love for all people.

Questions for Reflection: What has God taught you through your participation in a funeral? How did the environment and the engagement of your senses function as means for God to teach you?

Prayer: God of my salvation, you help me to know your ways and you teach me your paths. Send your Holy Spirit to lead me to your truth. Open for me the teachings of Jesus Christ, your Son. I wait for you all day long. You are God, for ever and ever. Amen.

Journal: Apply the phrase "less is more" to a recent experience of liturgical worship that you have had. What was the "less"? What was the "more"? What did God teach you?

Gospel Readings

1. REVELATION

See also Part I: Funeral Rites, 2. Related Rites and Prayers, Gathering in the Presence of the Body, Scripture Verse A: Spiritual Rest, and Part III: Texts of Sacred Scripture, 14. Funerals for Baptized Children, Gospel Readings, 1. Revealed to Infants.

Scripture: (Matt 11:25-30) [Jesus said,] "All things have been handed over to me by my Father; and no one knows the Son except the Father, and no one knows the Father except the Son and anyone to whom the Son chooses to reveal him" (11:27).

Order of Christian Funerals: par. 22.

Reflection: Who is God? Contrary to popular opinion, that is not a question which can be answered easily. Before Jesus, God was conceptualized in various ways: creator, judge, demander of animal sacrifices, law-giver. Jesus, however, caused people to rethink their understanding of God. Both Matthew's Gospel (11:25-27) and Luke's Gospel (10:21-22) portray Jesus as offering a prayer which answers the question, "Who is God?"

Jesus calls God "Father," a title which expresses the relationship of sons and daughters to their dad. "Father" implies intimacy and immanence instead of aloofness and transcendence. According to Jesus, God trusts people, especially Jesus, to whom God has handed over all. The theme of God entrusting all to Jesus is picked up later by the author of Matthew's Gospel in the narrative of the judgment of the nations (25:31-46) in which Jesus separates the sheep, the righteous, from the goats, those who did not do God's will.

Just as God trusts people, so people should trust God, like they trust their fathers. God provides for all our needs. In his first sermon (5:1–7:29), the Matthean Jesus tells us that our heavenly

Father knows that we need food, drink, and clothing. But we are instructed not to worry, to seek God's righteousness, and all those things will be given to us (6:25-34).

Jesus' answer of "Father" to the question "Who is God?" displays the special knowledge that Father and Son have of each other. People share this knowledge through Jesus, the One who reveals what God is like, who God is to and for us. Jesus serves as the mediator, the open valve on the pipeline of knowledge flowing from us to him and from him to God.

Ultimately, what Jesus reveals is that God is where people are. God speaks not on any inaccessible mountain top or in heaven, but in the lives of people, in their needs, sorrows, fears, and hopes. By listening to our authentic selves, the voice within us, we hear God.

We call the process of listening to God "discernment." We attempt to determine if we are hearing the voice of God or our own selfish words. If it is God's voice, we try to act on what we have heard. If it is not the voice of God, we clean up our own desires and prepare the way for God to be heard clearly. As long as we discover that what we hear and act on flows from and back to Jesus and what he taught and the way he lived, we can be sure that we are knowing God and receiving God's revelation.

The funeral of a child who died before baptism presents the occasion for us to remember that the child belongs to God through Jesus. The God whom Jesus revealed is a Father to all equally, baptized and unbaptized. The One who is manifested through the Scriptures and in the lives of those who listen to them is also revealed through death. Our needs, sorrows, fears, and hopes at the time of the funeral for a child enables us to call upon God as "Father" and to know even more intimately the love of our "Father" revealed to us in the death and resurrection of Jesus, God's Son.

Questions for Reflection: How do you answer the question, "Who is God?" Is the God of your answer more immanent or transcendent? Explain.

Prayer: God, my Father, you have handed over all things to your Son, Jesus Christ, and made him the way of knowing you. In all of the experiences of my life, help me to discern your word and your will. Strengthen my faith that one day I may see you face to face. I ask this through the Lord Jesus Christ and the Holy Spirit, one God, for ever and ever. Amen.

Journal: What contemporary image do you think can be used to describe Jesus as a mediator between God and people? In what ways has God been where you are, that is, in your needs, sorrows, fears, and hopes?

2. WITNESS

Scripture: (Mark 15:33-46) When it was noon, darkness came over the whole land until three in the afternoon. . . . Then Jesus gave a loud cry and breathed his last. And the curtain of the temple was torn in two, from top to bottom. Now when the centurion, who stood facing him, saw that in this way he breathed his last, he said, "Truly this man was God's Son!"

There were also women looking on from a distance; among them were Mary Magdalene, and Mary the mother of James the younger and of Joses, and Salome. These used to follow him and provided for him when he was in Galilee; and there were many other women who had come up with him to Jerusalem (15:33, 37-41).

Order of Christian Funerals: par. 22.

Reflection: Witnesses are people who tell what they believe to be the truth. In a legal sense, witnesses testify under oath to what they think is true. While we must consider each witness's biases and handicaps, in general, witnesses attest to the facts as best as they can.

The account of Jesus' death in Mark's Gospel presents three witnesses. Each attests to faith in Jesus at the time of his death. First, there is the torn curtain in the temple. The curtain, which separated the worshipers from God has been rent in two, states the author of Mark's Gospel. To put it another way, God has escaped. God has been set free. God's reign has begun with the death of God's Son, Jesus.

The torn-curtain detail in Mark's death narrative is meant to echo the torn heavens at Jesus' baptism by John in the Jordan (1:9-11). Just as Jesus was coming up out of the water, "he saw the heavens torn apart and the Spirit descending like a dove on him" (1:10). The author is telling the reader that God, who lives above the firmament, has come to the earth, the middle level of a three-storied universe, and that God's reign has begun. In both the torn-curtain scene and the torn-heavens scene, Mark's Gospel declares that God is where people presumed God not to be—nailed to a cross planted in the earth or standing in the middle of a river.

Second, the centurion bears witness to faith by declaring Jesus to be God's Son. In only two other places does the author of Mark's Gospel declare Jesus to be God's Son (with the exception of the title of his work at 1:1). After he is baptized and the heavens are torn apart, Jesus hears the voice from heaven saying, "You are my Son, the Beloved . . ." (1:11). After he is transfigured, a cloud overshadows

Jesus and his companions "and from the cloud there came a voice, 'This is my Son, the Beloved . . .'" (9:7).

Throughout Mark's Gospel, no disciple ever declares Jesus to be God's Son. That is the irony of the author's portrayal of a Roman pagan making the declaration and the reader waiting for one of the disciples to figure it out. In Markan theology, the baptism and voice set Jesus on a course of powerful words and deeds. That course is altered with the transfiguration and its voice which puts Jesus on a journey to Jerusalem during which he teaches the way of powerlessness. That God prefers the way of powerlessness is confirmed by the centurion's declaration of faith.

Third, a trio of women—Mary Magdalene, Mary the mother of James and Joses, and Salome—are among those who witness Jesus' death from a distance. They reappear later in the narrative at 16:1, making a trip to the tomb to anoint Jesus' body after the Sabbath. As women in the ancient world, they have no credibility; only men were reliable witnesses. Again, with a stroke of his ironic pen, the author of Mark's Gospel portrays the trio of women as the first witnesses of the resurrection. They receive the message that God has raised Jesus from the dead.

The same paradoxical witness occurs during funerals for children who died before they were baptized. In the face of death, we proclaim the paschal mystery—the passing over through death to life. We witness to our faith that death is but a passageway to new life; it is not the end of life. Death is ripped in two, like a curtain, to reveal God's reign of life. We remember the dead and all others who have died with the hope of seeing them again in heaven after we cross over death to life, like Jesus, the Son of God.

We bear witness to the Christian life by our lifestyle; how we live and how we die discloses our faith. Like the three women standing at a distance, by our example of living, others see us and know we are followers of the One who died and was raised to life again by God. Our lives witness what we believe to be the truth.

Questions for Reflection: How does your life witness your faith? Give specific examples. How is a funeral an opportunity for members of the Christian community to witness their faith? Give specific examples of how that can be done.

Prayer: God of heaven and earth, with the centurion at the foot of the cross I declare my faith in Jesus, your only-begotten Son. Strengthen me with the presence of your Holy Spirit. Guide me in your ways that, like the three women at the tomb, I may hear and bear witness to the good news of the resurrection of Jesus Christ, who lives and reigns with you and the Holy Spirit, one God, for ever and ever. Amen.

Journal: When have you experienced a torn curtain or torn heavens, discovering that God was present where you didn't expect God to be? When have you experienced the confirmation that God prefers the way of powerlessness, like the centurion's declaration at the foot of the cross? When have you been the recipient of the good news of new life on the other side of the grave, like the trio of women at Jesus' tomb?

3. HUMANITY REDEEMED

See also Part III: Texts of Sacred Scripture, 14. Funerals for Baptized Children, Gospel Readings, 6. Mother.

Scripture: (John 19:25-30) . . . [W]hen Jesus knew that all was now finished, he said (in order to fulfill the scripture), "I am thirsty." A jar full of sour wine was standing there. So they put a sponge full of the wine on a branch of hyssop and held it to his mouth. When Jesus had received the wine, he said, "It is finished." Then he bowed his head and gave up his spirit (19:28-30).

Order of Christian Funerals: par. 1.

Reflection: All of humanity has been redeemed by the death and resurrection of Christ. All people have been brought back to God through the sacrifice of Christ's death. Like the passover lamb was sacrificed and its blood sprinkled with hyssop on the lintel and doorposts of the houses of the Israelites, Jesus died on the cross, his blood sprinkled on the wood, becoming a new passover lamb, the perfect sacrifice surpassing all others. The old lamb reminded the people of their escape from Egyptian slavery to freedom; the new lamb reminds us of our escape from death to eternal life.

We call the death and resurrection of Christ the paschal mystery. It involves suffering, both the physical pain of being nailed to the wood of the cross and the spiritual pain of thirsting for the faith of people. It involves death, the handing over of the self to God, trusting that God will receive us. Resurrection is that climactic moment when he who had finished the work entrusted to him by God and fallen asleep in death was immediately awakened by God to new life. The ascension dimension of the paschal mystery, while being another way to speak of resurrection, connotes the rejoining of the second invisible person of the Trinity to the Godhead. There was never a time when Christ was not joined to the Godhead, but because he became human and entered into time, we need a metaphor to speak about his leaving time and entering into timelessness.

The author of John's Gospel portrays Jesus' death as the completion of his paschal mystery. Particularly important is the mention of the jar of sour wine. We heard about six jars of water-become-wine in the story of the wedding feast at Cana. There, Jesus' hour had not yet come. The astute reader has been waiting since chapter two of John's Gospel for the appearance of the seventh jar of wine, the completion of Jesus' mission, the arrival of his hour. Finally, immediately before his last words and his death, his hour arrives. The wine is sour to represent the crucifixion and the death of the Son of God, but his work is complete. The paschal mystery has been established.

Because we are redeemed, we celebrate the paschal mystery at the time of the funeral for a child who died before baptism. We entrust the child to God's all-embracing love, like Jesus entrusted himself to God. We believe that the child, who has suffered and died, has passed over in imitation of Jesus. We believe that the child has entered into the wedding feast of heaven where the wine never turns sour and never runs out. In the short life of the child, the paschal mystery has been traced, and we recognize that even though one was not ritually baptized, God has supplied all that was needed through the paschal mystery of Christ.

Questions for Reflection: In what ways do you find the paschal mystery—suffering, death, new life—traced in your life now? How do you think your experiences now will help you face final death?

Prayer: God of Jesus, I bow my head in worship. Through the death and resurrection of your Son, Jesus Christ, you have established the paschal mystery and redeemed all of humanity. Trace in my life the lines of your love. Help me to faithfully follow in the footsteps of Jesus, suffering, dying, and rising with him, who lives and reigns with you and the Holy Spirit, one God, for ever and ever. Amen.

Journal: In what ways do you think Jesus is like a passover lamb? In what ways do you think a dead child is like a passover lamb? What do you mean when you say that Christ redeemed humanity?

16. Antiphons and Psalms

A selection of five psalms, appropriate for use in funerals for infants and children, has been made from the sixteen choices provided in Part III, Section 16. Antiphons and Psalms, of the *Order of Christian Funerals*.

2. YOUTH

See also Part III: Texts of Sacred Scripture, 14. Funerals for Baptized Children, Responsorial Psalms, 2. Fear, and 15. Funerals for Children Who Died Before Baptism, Responsorial Psalm: Teach Me Your Ways.

Scripture: (Ps 25)

> Be mindful of your mercy, O LORD, and of your steadfast love,
>   for they have been from of old.
> Do not remember the sins of my youth or my transgressions;
>   according to your steadfast love remember me,
>   for your goodness' sake, O LORD! (25:6-7).

Order of Christian Funerals: par. 344.

Reflection: Psalm 25 is appropriate for use during the funeral rites for a teenager. The psalmist asks God not to remember the failures of youth, but to remember the person singing the song or making the petition. Teens are more important than their actions from the psalmist's point of view.

The teen years are an almost uncontrollable time of life. The body is undergoing the transition from childhood to adulthood. As teens drink in experiences of living, they are not able to calculate the cost and end up taking risks which will make them shiver later in their lives. They explore their personal possibilities and try new things. Teens feel indestructible and act on this incomplete information.

The death of a teenager is devastating to both parents and peers, especially if death was the result of taking one too many risks. The daily papers contain stories about teens killed in automobile accidents because they were driving at excessive speeds or drinking or taking drugs or meeting a dare from a friend. We read about teens being shot in gang rumbles. Athletic teens, unaware of some physical problem, collapse on the field or the court and die from heart failure, a collapsed lung, or a brain malfunction. Some teens die as a result of cancer or AIDS after several years of struggling with the disease.

At the time of the death of a teenager, the mourners are directed to use the Scriptures, especially the psalms, and to call upon God's mercy and steadfast love for the dead teen and for themselves. As the psalmist makes clear, God is interested in remembering people, not in remembering the sins of their youth or their transgressions. Certainly, God's love is stronger than teenage failures. Certainly, God doesn't remember the foolishness of youth. God covers our teenage years with a love that is steadfast, enduring, and not affected by our youthful stupidity.

Adults have the responsibility continually to call teenagers to adulthood. Parental guidance is indispensable during the teen years, especially during the funeral rites for a peer. We do not overlook the risk that may have caused the death, but we help others to learn from it. We do not pretend that mourning is not necessary, we enter into it fully and experience the loss. Teens mourn in their own manner, but they need the support of adults and their counsel in learning from the experience. Over all, they need to be reminded of God's steadfast love for them and for the deceased teen, just as their parents, relatives, and friends remind them of their steadfast love for them.

Questions for Reflection: What sins, transgressions, or failures of your youth do you remember or wish you could change now? How did these help to shape you and your life, help to make you a better person? How did God's steadfast love for you guide you and teach you?

Prayer: Steadfast and loving God, through the experiences of my life, you help me to know your ways and to walk in the paths of your truth. Remember your mercy, which has existed from of old, and do not remember the failures of my youth. Remember me in heaven, where you live and reign with your Son, Jesus Christ, and the Holy Spirit, one God, for ever and ever. Amen.

Journal: Look through a paper for a news story or an obituary about a teenager who died. What does the teen's life teach you? What does the teen's death teach you? How can you help to teach those lessons to others?

7. GOD PROTECTS THE SIMPLE

Scripture: (Ps 116)

> Gracious is the LORD, and righteous;
>   our God is merciful.
> The LORD protects the simple;
>   when I was brought low, he saved me.

Return, O my soul, to your rest,
for the LORD has dealt bountifully with you (116:5-7).

Order of Christian Funerals: par. 241.

Reflection: The church makes a distinction between those children who died after being baptized and those who died before being baptized. The distinction is not made to separate people, but to plan the texts and elements of the funeral rites. We don't want to use signs and words which do not speak the truth or may contradict the truth. For example, we don't want to sprinkle water in remembrance of a baptism and utter prayers that mention a baptism that didn't take place, nor do we want to omit sprinkling water on the body of a child who was baptized. Authenticity is the key in planning the funeral rites for a child.

No matter which condition of the dead child influences the elements and texts of the funeral rites, we proclaim that God protects the simple. And infants and children are among the simple, those who do not yet lead complicated lives, unlike most adults.

The psalmist proclaims that God takes care of the simple in terms of the Holy One's characteristics. God's graciousness is sung about by the composer of the psalm; God shares God's self or essence with people and serves them. The Compassionate One is righteous, calling people to live according to God's ways. God is merciful, ready to show kindness and forgive human failings. The psalmist says that God saves, rescuing people from what might harm them. And over all these characteristics, God is bountiful, unlimited, rich in what matters the most.

We can rest in comfort in the midst of God's benevolence. The dead can rest in the salvation God offers. God is gracious, righteous, and merciful to the dead infant or child. Out of God's bountiful love, we can be confident that God protects the simple. We can enter into God's rest.

Questions for Reflection: In what ways are you simple? In what ways are you complicated? For each category identify how God has been bountiful to you.

Prayer: Gracious God, your never-ending mercy never ceases to call me to righteousness. Protect me in my simplicity, and help me to find rest from the complications of my life. Out of your bountiful love, send me your Holy Spirit, and raise me from death to new life with Jesus Christ, your Son, who lives and reigns with you for ever and ever. Amen.

Journal: In what ways has God been gracious, righteous, and merciful to you? How does such a bounty make you feel? If you have known an infant or child who died, how does knowing that God protects the simple help you cope with the death?

9. BLAMELESS

Scripture: (Ps 119:1-8)

> Happy are those whose way is blameless,
>   who walk in the law of the LORD.
> Happy are those who keep his decrees,
>   who seek him with their whole heart,
> who also do no wrong,
>   but walk in his ways (119:1-3).

Order of Christian Funerals: par. 246.

Reflection: Certainly, infants and children are blameless, without fault or responsibility for their actions unless they have attained the age of reason. Only when we have attained the ability to reason, to distinguish clearly between right and wrong, can we be held accountable morally for our actions. Therefore, in the words of the psalmist we can say that infants and children walked in God's law, kept God's decrees, and sought God with their whole heart. In other words, infants and children did no wrong and walked in God's ways in a manner fitting them, since God draws all to God's self.

During the vigil service for a deceased infant or child, a family member or friend may speak in remembrance of the infant's or child's blamelessness. The person verbalizes for those present the personality and habits, the unique characteristics of the little one, and helps all know how the infant or child enriched the family and left an imprint on it.

The experience of the chaos which accompanies the death of an infant or a child challenges the ordering of life as it is created in the Hebrew Bible (Old Testament) Book of Genesis and which is reordered by God's law given to Moses on Mount Sinai. Chaos creates alienation and a feeling of abandonment. Family and friends do not think that they can continue to live without the infant or child.

Through God's word in the Scriptures and through the words spoken in remembrance of the infant or child by another person, we hear God promise order to our lives as we strive to walk in God's ways, following Jesus who died and was raised by God to new life. God loves us and searches for us even as we seek God with our whole heart.

Questions for Reflection: In what ways do you think "blameless" adequately characterizes an infant or a child? What other words would you use to describe the blameless state of an infant or a child? Define each word.

Prayer: Blameless God, through the law, you taught your people to walk in your ways, to keep your decrees, and to seek you with all their heart. Through the death and resurrection of Jesus, you have revealed your great love for me and reordered the chaos of the world. Strengthen me with your Holy Spirit to remain faithful to his teaching. Hear me through Jesus Christ the Lord. Amen.

Journal: From your own experience of infants and children, at what age do you think they reach the age of reason and can be held responsible morally for their actions? How can you tell when children are able to make decisions and to be held accountable for them and their consequences?

11. PEACE WITHIN

Scripture: (Ps 122)

> I was glad when they said to me,
>> "Let us go to the house of the LORD!"
> Our feet are standing within your gates, O Jerusalem.
> . . . .
> Pray for the peace of Jerusalem:
>> "May they prosper who love you.
> Peace be within your walls,
>> and security within your towers."
> For the sake of my relatives and friends
>> I will say, "Peace be within you."
> For the sake of the house of the LORD our God,
>> I will seek your good (122:1-2, 6-9).

Order of Christian Funerals: par. 242.

Reflection: It is easy to wish people the gift of peace, but it is not always so easy to attain it. Peace is not the absence of war, but contentment, wholeness before God, prosperity in God's presence. Standing before God, we are aware of who we are and who God is, and that brings security, happiness, peace. We seek not only our own good but that of our neighbors as well, and that brings peace. In the midst of the chaos of the death of a loved one, peace is not cheap.

However, peace is an important aspect of the funeral rites, especially for those of a child and/or when children are members of the assembly. The chaos surrounding the death of an infant or a child can be dealt with in some degree through planning. The sisters, brothers, friends, classmates of the child should be kept in mind as the texts, readings, music, gestures, processions, and silences are selected and planned. The reality of death is not to be covered up, as in pretending that the deceased child is not really dead. But if death is approached from a peaceful point of view by the planners and the minister, who may offer brief remarks to the children, the funeral rites for a child can become the occasion for an experience of God's peace.

The dead child has arrived in the new Jerusalem, where peace reigns, where God lives. The peace we experience here is but a glimpse of the peace to come. The glimpse of peace in this life is nothing in comparison to the security, happiness, and prosperity that await us beyond the grave.

Children attending the funeral of a child should be invited to participate in music that enables them to say farewell to their deceased friend through song. They can be invited to help place the pall on the coffin, to present Christian signs that honor the memory of the deceased child. Children can be invited to walk around the coffin during the processions. And silence may offer them the opportunity to pause and think about the various aspects of the funeral rites. All serve to foster a sense of peace in children, a peace that is but a momentary view of what the fullness of God's peace will be like.

Questions for Reflection: How do you experience peace now? Where do you find it? How does peace make you feel?

Prayer: God of Jerusalem, in your house I find peace. Grant me the gifts of prosperity, security, and friends. Open for me the gates of your city where you live and reign in the peace of the Holy Spirit with your Son, the Lord Jesus Christ, for ever and ever. Amen.

Journal: If you have participated in the funeral for a child, how was the chaos of death dealt with through the funeral rites? If you have not attended the funeral for a child, how do you think the chaos of death could be dealt with through the funeral rites?

14. OUT OF THE DEPTHS

See also Part IV: Office for the Dead, 18. Evening Prayer, Second Psalm: Watch for Morning.

Scripture: (Ps 130)

> Out of the depths I cry to you, O LORD.
>   LORD, hear my voice!

Let your ears be attentive
to the voice of my supplications!

. . . .

O Israel, hope in the LORD! (130:1-2, 7a)

Order of Christian Funerals: par. 244.

Reflection: The composer of Psalm 130 looks deep inside the self and enters into that dimension where all honesty is laid bare. Out of the depths of one's self, from the inner core of a person's being, the psalmist cries to God and pleads that his or her voice be heard. The person feels like one is submerged in the deeps of the ocean.

The depths, one's inner reality, is the place to which one retreats when challenged or confronted with the chaos accompanying the death of an infant or a child, or anyone else for that matter. From within we beg that God will be attentive and listen to our cries coming from our hearts.

The death of an infant or a child can send the parents and other members of the family to those depths which may be released as a fountain of tears or mournful sighs, particularly when the body of the infant or child is received at the church as part of the vigil or when the family views the body for the first time. The vigil, the first major prayer of the funeral rites, acknowledges the reality of death and the pain of separation which it causes. If the body is not brought to the church for the vigil, the greeting, song, invitation to prayer, and opening prayer serve the same purpose—to declare that death is an aspect of life. All human life on earth is temporary; we are merely passing through.

A child who died violently due to an accident, a drive-by shooting, or abuse of some kind makes the funeral rites even more difficult because we seek answers to our questions: Why did this happen? What could we have done to prevent it? Why did it have to be this child who died?

All we can do is enter into the questions without having immediate answers to them. We hear the words of the psalmist pleading for help and make those words our own. We have hope in God, who hears us and directs our lives. Sometimes hope materializes, becomes flesh, in terms of sparking the community to solve some of the problems that lead to the violent death of infants and children. Before anything is done, however, we must search the depths of our selves in all honesty. From the core of our being we will find the strength of God, who is attentive to our needs, gives us hope, and moves us to action.

Questions for Reflection: When did you most recently retreat to the depths of your being? Why did you go there? With what were you being challenged? What hope did you find there from God?

Prayer: Attentive God, out of the depths of my inner self I call to you, confident that you listen to my pleas for strength. Help me to realize the shortness of life and how quickly it can disappear. Give me the hope of sharing in your eternal life with your Son, the Lord Jesus Christ, and the Holy Spirit, one God, for ever and ever. Amen.

Journal: Do you live your life as if you are merely passing through or as if you are here to stay? What specific aspects of your lifestyle support your answer to the previous question?

PART IV

Office for the Dead

The vigil may take the form of a liturgy of the word . . . or of some part of the office for the dead. . . .

The vigil may be celebrated at a convenient time in the home of the deceased child, in the funeral home, parlor or chapel of rest, or in some other suitable place.

Whenever possible, ministers should involve the family of the deceased in the planning of the hour and in the designation of ministers.

—*Order of Christian Funerals,* pars. 243, 244, 371.

17. Morning Prayer

Order of Christian Funerals: par. 367.

FIRST PSALM: LAMENT AND PETITION

Scripture: (Ps 51)

> Have mercy on me, O God,
>   according to your steadfast love
>
> . . . .
>
> Create in me a clean heart, O God,
>   and put a new and right spirit within me.
>
> . . . .
>
> O Lord, open my lips,
>   and my mouth will declare your praise (51:1a, 10, 15).

Order of Christian Funerals: par. 357.

Reflection: The word "lament," etymologically associated with the sounds of the words "loon" and "barking," means to mourn aloud or to wail. A lament is the way we express our sorrow in a demonstrable way, such as crying out in grief.

A petition is an earnest request or entreaty. We make a formal request of someone to help us in a particular matter. Usually during prayer, our petition is made to God for others' needs and our own.

Psalm 51 contains both of these elements, lament and petition, as well as praise, and, thus, is appropriate for Morning Prayer for a dead infant or child.

The mourning done by parents and friends can appropriately be called "lamenting." They express their sorrow in various ways, such as standing near the coffin and greeting friends, talking about the infant or child and the circumstances of the death, shedding tears, clinging to the infant's or child's favorite toy.

Following the lead of Psalm 51, prayerful lament moves us to petition. We ask God to have mercy on the dead and the living according to God's unfailing love. We need a bulwark, some type of support, and God's love is it. Requesting that God create a clean heart in us, one not preoccupied with things, we seek to be genuine in our stance before God. We beg God to put new spirit within us, to give new life to us, and to provide new life for the infant or child on the other side of death.

The last movement of Psalm 51 is praise. We ask God to enable us to praise God. We cannot offer praise alone. So, we beg that God will open our lips and put the right words in our mouths, even as we grieve.

The words of Psalm 51, gently guiding us from lament and petition to praise, help to instill confidence in those who grieve the loss of an infant or a child. As family members and friends acknowledge their sorrow and lament the dead, they ask the God of life for help in strengthening their hope in eternal life. For such an undeserved gift, we praise the eternal God.

Questions for Reflection: What recent experiences have you had of lamenting and petitioning? Who or what did you lament? Whom did you petition? How did your experiences lead you to praise?

Prayer: Steadfast God, you comfort me in my sorrow. Create a clean heart in me and set me on fire with the love of your Holy Spirit. Deepen my hope of praising you for ever in heaven, where you live and reign with the Lord Jesus Christ for ever and ever. Amen.

Journal: What do you think is the connection between the sounds of the words "lament," "loon," "barking"? How does that connection help you understand the connection between "lament" and "petition"?

CANTICLE: PROCLAIM FAITHFULNESS

Scripture: (Isa 38:10-14, 17-20)

> I said: In the noontide of my days
> I must depart. . . .
>
> . . . .
> I said, I shall not see the LORD
>   in the land of the living;
> I shall look upon mortals no more
>   among the inhabitants of the world.
>
> . . . .
> The living, the living, they thank you [O Lord],
>   as I do this day;
> fathers make known to children
>   your faithfulness.
> The LORD will save me,
>   and we will sing to stringed instruments
> all the days of our lives
>   at the house of the LORD (38:10a, 11, 19-20).

Order of Christian Funerals: pars. 369, 370.

Reflection: In chapter 38 of his book, the prophet Isaiah records the prayer of a king. After being sick and recovering, King Hezekiah praised God for God's faithfulness. The king of Judah was at the point of death, in the noontime or midday of his life. He regretted no longer "seeing God," a reference to the Temple in Jerusalem, where God had decided to live with people in the inner sanctuary of that building, called the Holy of Holies. If he died, Hezekiah knew that he would no longer gaze upon other people, either. He would go to the land of the dead.

However, the king did not die; he recovered. In thanksgiving for his recovery, he offered a prayer to God and praised God for faithfulness and for saving him from death. When reciting or singing Hezekiah's canticle during the Office for the Dead, we are reminded that parents share with their children the same faithfulness of God that Hezekiah sang about. Indeed, just as parents are loyal and devoted to their children, so is God firm in adhering to God's covenant with people. Our God is interested in life—not death.

During the funeral rites for an infant or a child, Hezekiah's words offer comfort to the mourners and point toward a greater truth. Not only does God heal our illness, like God did for the king, but through the resurrection of Jesus, God has revealed life on the other side of the grave. Unlike the king, who lamented that he would not be able to see God, Jesus revealed that we can see God in the land of the dead (which is really another land of the living) and that we need not fear passing through death to begin life in a new way. That's what life is all about anyway, isn't it? Life is about beginning over and over again until we begin it eternally in God's presence.

No matter whether we pray in the funeral home or funeral parlor, a chapel or a church, and no matter how we adapt the Office for the Dead to reflect the circumstances of the death of the infant or child, Isaiah's record of Hezekiah's prayer moves us to praise God for God's faithfulness and to proclaim to others how God is faithful all the days of our lives here on earth and all the days of our lives in the land of the eternally living on the other side of death.

Questions for Reflection: In what ways has God demonstrated faithfulness to you? How does each of these strengthen your faith in eternal life on the other side of death?

Prayer: Faithful God, you never abandon me in my sickness. Through the resurrection of your Son, Jesus Christ, you reveal that even though I pass through death, I will discover eternal life. For such great faithfulness I join those on earth and in heaven in praising you eternally: Father, Son, and Holy Spirit, one God, for ever and ever. Amen.

Journal: What is your philosophy of life? How does it compare and contrast to that of King Hezekiah? (The king's story and prayer can be found in Isaiah 38:1-22.)

SECOND PSALM: A. LIFE-LONG PRAISE

Scripture: (Ps 146)

> Praise the LORD!
> Praise the LORD, O my soul!
> I will praise the LORD as long as I live;
>   I will sing praises to my God all my life long.
>
> . . . .
> Happy are those whose help is the God of Jacob,
>   whose hope is in the LORD their God,
> who made heaven and earth,
>   the sea, and all that is in them;
> who keeps faith forever. . . (146:1-2, 5-6).

Order of Christian Funerals: par. 372.

Reflection: Husbands and wives often praise each other for finishing a task, saying, "Honey, you did that very well." Teachers praise students, declaring, "You did an excellent job on that assignment." Sometimes, students praise their teachers: "You are my favorite teacher in the whole world." Co-workers praise each other, stating, "You worked hard on that deal and deserve a bonus."

The psalmist praises God. Unlike our momentary words of approval, the singer of the psalm praises God's help all the days of his or her life. As long as the person lives, the writer wants to praise God, the creator of heaven, earth, sea, and all life everywhere.

Particularly singled out for praise is God's faithfulness. Husbands and wives are faithful to each other, as are teachers devoted to their students and co-workers to employees, but we falter, make mistakes, and fail. God doesn't. God is faithful for ever and deserves our life-long praise.

When praying the Office for the Dead during the funeral rites for an infant or a child, it is a good time to recall the parents' faithfulness to their child, even if death was the result of negligence, violence, or abuse. This is not an effort to remove the guilt of the parents, but, certainly, those who conceived life, brought it to birth, and nurtured it for a period of time had some sense of faithfulness, no matter how they failed.

It is also a good time to recall God's faithfulness to us both now and beyond the grave. Even though we may think that God has abandoned us or the dead infant or child, God hasn't. Human failure or inability to save from miscalculation, disease, or violence does not reflect on God. Through his resurrection, Jesus revealed that God is faithful through death to new life.

Such faithfulness is best proclaimed through the singing of the psalms both in the Office for the Dead and those chosen as responses to Scripture passages in the other funeral rites. The psalms are ancient Hebrew songs. Singing a song, instead of reciting its lyrics, emphasizes the nature of the prayer and it brings people into closer union with each other. Through singing, people are united in heart, mind, and words in praise of God.

Questions for Reflection: What experiences have you had of reciting and singing psalms? Did you discover that those who prayed the psalms were more united when they sang or recited them? Explain.

Prayer: God, creator of heaven, earth, and sea and all that is in them, I give you praise for all that you have made. Inspire me with your Holy Spirit to praise your faithfulness all my life long. Fill me with the hope of praising you beyond the grave in heaven with your Son, Jesus Christ, in the unity of the Holy Spirit, for ever and ever. Amen.

Journal: Write your own psalm of praise for God's faithfulness all your life long. Use Psalm 146 as a model, or use the music to one of your favorite songs and write your own lyrics of praise.

SECOND PSALM: B. PRAISE GOD!

Scripture: (Ps 150)

> Praise the LORD!
> Praise God in his sanctuary;
>   praise him in his mighty firmament!
> Praise him for his mighty deeds;
>   praise him according to his surpassing greatness!
>
> . . . .
> Let everything that breathes praise the LORD! (150:1-2, 6a).

Order of Christian Funerals: par. 359.

Reflection: There is no end to our praise of God, as the author of Psalm 150 makes clear. The psalmist sings about praising God in God's dwelling place on earth, the Temple or sanctuary where the Jews worshiped God for hundreds of years until it was destroyed by the Romans in 70 C.E.

Besides praising God in God's house, the psalmist praises God in the firmament, in ancient cosmology that place above the dome of the sky, God's permanent home above the terrarium-like Hebrew conception of the earth. From God's house, God controlled everything in the universe.

God's mighty deeds are praised, too. In Israelite mentality, God's mightiest deed was the exodus from Egypt. By their escape, the people of Israel left slavery behind and embraced a new and free way of life. Also included in God's mighty deeds would be the second exodus, the Israelites leaving the land of Babylonian captivity and returning to the land of Judah. Not to be missed, of course, in listing God's mighty deeds, is the way God directed world history to the benefit of his people.

In praising God's surpassing greatness, the psalmist acknowledges God to be above all of creation, beyond the vastness of the universe, inconceivable for the human mind. God is supreme.

When celebrating the funeral rites for an infant or a child, such loud praise may at first seem out of place, and, depending upon the circumstances of the death of the infant or child, may be inappropriate. That is why the church permits the use of other psalms in the Office for the Dead. As long as they are chosen in relation to the time of day they will be prayed and for their suitability for use in the Office for the Dead, any may be chosen from the 150 psalms. Especially recommended are those found in Part III of the *Order of Christian Funerals.*

The praise of God is appropriate as the mourners recall that the dead infant or child has passed through death to eternal life with God where the praise of God never ends. This understanding gives the psalm's words, "Let everything that breathes praise God," a new understanding. Indeed, not only everything on this side of the grave that has the breath of life praises God, but all that lives on the other side of the grave and breathes eternally of God's Spirit praises the All-holy One. The whole universe is united in one gigantic, unending chorus of praise.

Questions for Reflection: What place (such as a church, prayer corner, room) is most conducive for you to praise God? For what mighty deeds in your life do you praise God? Make a list and pray it as a litany of praise.

Prayer: Everything that breathes praises your name, God of heaven and earth. I join my voice to those who have gone before me in faith and with those who share this small planet in thanking you for your mighty deeds in my life. Be my help and guide through this life and fill me with the breath of eternal life. Your greatness surpasses my every thought as I praise you, Father, Son, and Holy Spirit, perfect Trinity, for ever and ever. Amen.

Journal: Why do you think praise of God is appropriate during the funeral rites for an infant or a child? Besides Psalm 150, what other psalms do you think could be appropriately included in the Office for the Dead prayed for an infant or a child? Look through the Book of Psalms in your Bible, choose one, and reflect on its meaning for you.

READING: ASLEEP IN CHRIST

See also part III: Texts of Sacred Scripture, 14. Funerals for Baptized Children, New Testament Readings, 5. Encouragement.

Scripture: (1 Thess 4:14) . . . [S]ince we believe that Jesus died and rose again, even so, through Jesus, God will bring with him those who have died (4:14).

Order of Christian Funerals: par. 360.

Reflection: The metaphor for death that we use the most is sleep. It is appropriate, since every night we lay down, cover up, and enter into unconsciousness. Sleep is as close to death as we can come without actually dying. In Eucharistic Prayer I, we remember "those who have died and [who] have gone before us marked with the sign of faith" and pray that "all who sleep in Christ [will] find . . . light, happiness, and peace" in God's presence.

A caution is in order here. When speaking about death to children, we should not use the metaphor of sleep for death. Adults who tell children while viewing the body, "Grandpa is sleeping," can unconsciously instill fear of going to sleep in their children. A child reasons that if grandpa falls asleep and never wakes up in this life, the child does not want to fall asleep and not wake up. The child will not want to go to bed.

In the oldest New Testament piece of literature we possess, Paul uses the metaphor of sleep for death in his first letter to the Thessalonians. In his understanding, Jesus fell asleep in death on the cross, but God awakened him to new life through the resurrection. Likewise, writes Paul, we who believe in Jesus and fall asleep in death will be awakened by God to new life. Death, falling asleep, is followed by resurrection, waking up.

Paul, who like us does not know of what resurrection consists—because it is beyond our realm of experience—believes that life is reborn (another metaphor for death), made new, on the other side of death. Just like we wake up each morning renewed after a good night's sleep, we will wake up after dying and experience total renewal. We don't fear going to bed and falling asleep. In fact, we look forward to the pleasure we receive crawling under the covers, snuggling up on our favorite pillow, and entering the world of dreams. We should not fear death, either. It is a means to beginning life in a new way. It is an aspect of what real living is all about. Life is changed by death, but it is not ended.

During the Office for the Dead of an infant, a child, or a teen, a longer passage from Scripture may be used, such as 1 Thessalonians 4:13-18, which further explains Paul's metaphorical use of sleeping/awakening for death/resurrection. Also, another reading from a nonbiblical source may follow the biblical passage. However, it should communicate some Christian truth about the paschal mystery of Christ—his death and resurrection—and our Christian hope of sharing in it.

A nonbiblical reading might be taken from a favorite author of the parents of the dead infant, child, or teen, his or her favorite story, or a passage or poem of the dead's peers. The point is to use a metaphor to communicate our faith that what God did for Jesus— awaken him from death to new life—God will do for us.

Questions for Reflection: Besides the metaphor sleeping/awakening, what others do you use for death? Identify how each communicates your faith and hope for new life on the other side of death.

Prayer: God of Jesus, I believe that you raised your Son from the dead and bestowed upon him eternal life. May all my relatives and friends who have fallen asleep in Christ find in your presence light, happiness, and peace. Trace in my life the sign of faith, and, after I fall asleep in death, awaken me to the new life you share with Jesus Christ and the Holy Spirit, one God, for ever and ever. Amen.

Journal: What nonbiblical stories, passages, poems do you treasure as vehicles of communicating the paschal mystery and Christian hope? Include references to these in your journal along with an explanation of why each is important to you.

CANTICLE OF ZECHARIAH: REDEEMED

Scripture: (Luke 1:68-79) . . . Zechariah was filled with the Holy Spirit and spoke this prophecy:

"Blessed be the Lord God of Israel,
for he has looked favorably on his people and redeemed
them.

He has raised up a mighty savior for us
    in the house of his servant David,
as he spoke through the mouth of his holy prophets from of old,
    that we would be saved from our enemies and from the hand
    of all who hate us" (1:67-71).

Order of Christian Funerals: par. 362.

Reflection: The verb "to redeem" means "to buy back." In a consumer
culture like ours, it most often refers to the coupons we clip from the
newspaper or other source and redeem, meaning we get thirty-five,
fifty, or seventy-five cents off the total cost of a product we pur-
chase; we trade a piece of paper for a small amount off the total cost
of a box of cereal. Redeem can also refer to a trophy won back by a
team in competitive sports; for instance, in a championship game, a
high school basketball team wins back the state trophy lost last
year to an opposing team. A paid ransom can redeem a person from
the distress of captivity; through intense negotiations, presidents
and kings reach peace settlements between countries and people
caught in the middle are set free. In Christianity, "to redeem"
means "to free from the consequences of sin"; what human beings
could not do for themselves, God did for them through the death
and resurrection of Jesus.

Zechariah's canticle, unique to Luke's Gospel, praises God for
redeeming people through Jesus. God favored people so much that
Jesus became a human being and redeemed us from the consequences of our feeble, human state—our inability to be perfect,
called sin. Through Zechariah's words, the author of Luke's Gospel
proclaims that God has saved us through the One from David's
house.

Luke chooses David as Jesus' ancestor because he is the epit-
ome of the type of warrior-king expected by the Jewish people of the
first century C.E. The Jews had been oppressed by foreign occupa-
tion forces successively from Babylon, Persia, Greece, and Rome.
The prophets had longed for deliverance from these powers, called
enemies, but the result was usually the imposition of more taxes
with different rulers sitting on thrones in far-away countries de-
manding allegiance from their vassal Jewish territory.

The irony in Zechariah's thanksgiving for redemption is that
Jesus didn't fit the popular expectations of a savior. He was not a
warrior king; he preached love of enemies. He led no one into battle;
he started no wars, and at the most may have turned over a few
money-changers' tables. It is impossible to trace his lineage to

David if God is his father and Joseph isn't; he doesn't have the male connection needed in a Jewish genealogy.

The point Luke is making is that God chose to redeem us God's way and not our own. The death of an infant or a child offers us the opportunity, not only to remember that point, but to take confidence that the dead is redeemed by Jesus Christ, saved from the final enemy, death, and given eternal life beyond the grave. Through the death and resurrection of Jesus, God redeemed the world; certainly, that would not have been our way of doing it, but it was God's way. In the face of death, we stand in awe of how God saves us and praise God for such an undeserved gift.

Questions for Reflection: How do you define the verb "to redeem"? What are your experiences of "redemption"? How do your definition and your experiences give you hope when facing the death of a relative or friend?

Prayer: Blessed are you, God of all nations. Through the death and resurrection of your Son, you have looked favorably on all people and redeemed them. You have rescued them from death and given them eternal life. Make me worthy of your gracious gift. Strengthen my faith in the resurrection of Jesus Christ, who lives and reigns with you and the Holy Spirit, one God, for ever and ever. Amen.

Journal: Why do you think God chose the death and resurrection of Jesus as the means of redemption? How does the Holy Spirit help you understand God's ways of redeeming humanity?

18. Evening Prayer

Order of Christian Funerals: par. 243.

FIRST PSALM: YOUR KEEPER

Scripture: (Ps 121)

> I lift up my eyes to the hills—
>   from where will my help come?
> My help comes from the LORD,
>   who made heaven and earth
>
> . . . .
>   . . . [H]e who keeps you will not slumber.
> He who keeps Israel
>   will neither slumber nor sleep (121: 1-2, 3b-4).

Order of Christian Funerals: par. 358.

Reflection: We are safe in assuming that every evening most people go to bed and rest in the security of their homes. The doors are closed and locked, the children are tucked into bed with their own security blanket or stuffed toy. An infant's room may be equipped with an intercom or some type of baby minder which enables the parents in their room to hear the child if he or she awakens and begins to cry. No harm is expected because all is provided, and all is safe, and all is kept.

The psalmist uses an image similar to the security we feel in our homes to communicate trust in God. "Looking for help?" asks the lyrics of the psalm. "Look at the hills and the mountains—those places where God was thought to live." The psalmist continues, "The creator of heaven and earth helps us, keeps us, watches over us, like the ancient night watch patrolling the city walls, like the night watch at a cattle roundup in the old West, like a security guard at a warehouse." God never dozes off, never sleeps, never slumbers. And, according to the psalmist, that should make us feel secure.

During evening prayer, the church recommends that we sing Psalm 121 as daylight fades and the evening shadows descend. The psalms offers us security in the darkness of night, like that which children feel after their parents tuck them into bed and implant the last good-night kiss on their forehead. God takes care of us and watches out for us, like parents care for their children and protect them.

The psalm can also foster security in us as we face the final night, that is, death, for ourselves or with those we love. We entrust the dead to God, who promises eternal life on the other side of the grave. We trust that the One who never sleeps watches and protects the dead child. The security depicted by Psalm 121 is appropriate when the Office for the Dead is celebrated for infants, children, and teens. By praying it, we are reminded that God is the keeper of all people. God is the only source of perfect security.

Through praying Psalm 121, we lament death's darkness, and we petition God for light. But we are secure and confident that the dead already rests in God's reign. We trust that we will experience that security one day, too. Meanwhile we find comfort in knowing that God keeps us.

Questions for Reflection: In what ways has God been your keeper, the One who has helped you throughout your life? Call to mind specific instances when you knew God was watching out for you.

Prayer: God, my helper, you never fall asleep, but keep watch throughout the night to protect me. As I lift up my eyes to the hills,

I beg you to deepen my trust in you. When I fall asleep in death, raise me to eternal life, like you raised up your own Son, Jesus Christ, who lives and reigns with you and the Holy Spirit, one God, for ever and ever. Amen.

Journal: Locked doors, tucked into bed, and never sleeping are images of security. What other metaphors might be used to express the security we feel we have in God? Make a list and explain what aspect of security each communicates.

SECOND PSALM: WATCH FOR MORNING

See also Part III: Texts of Sacred Scripture, 16. Antiphons and Psalms, 14. Out of the Depths.

Scripture: (Ps 130)

> Out of the depths I cry to you, O LORD.
>   Lord, hear my voice!
> Let your ears be attentive
>   to the voice of my supplications!
>
> . . . .
> I wait for the LORD, my soul waits,
>   and in his word I hope;
> my soul waits for the Lord
>   more than those who watch for the morning,
>   more than those who watch for the morning (130:1-2, 5-6).

Order of Christian Funerals: par. 364.

Reflection: Most people have either heard about or read about the "big bang" theory of how the universe began. Basically, this scientific theory states that at some unknown point in time a giant cosmic explosion of a single mass of material sent stars and planets hurling into infinite space and the pieces are still flying apart. The "bang" doesn't refer to a sound, but to an explosion of light, immense and blinding. Keeping in mind that the "big bang" is a theory, we could also say that the universe began with a soft and quiet sigh which can still be heard in the breath of every living thing as well as in the wind that whispers throughout the universe.

Out of the depths of our sighing, we cry to God and beg to be heard during the funeral rites for an infant, a child, or a teen. We ask God to pay attention to our petitions for all those who have died marked with the sign of faith—the cross of Jesus. The sign of faith is traced on our foreheads before baptism. Parents may trace it on the heads of the children before they fall asleep at night or before they leave the house for school in the morning. We trace it over ourselves as a prayer which begins and ends a time of prayer. Priests and bishops mark it over us in liturgical blessings. In death we trace the sign of faith on the forehead of the deceased and over them as they wait to rise to final glory with Christ.

We, the living, wait because we do not know what is beyond death. We wait with hope that there is life, like the life God gave to Jesus by raising him from the dead. Our watching is like waiting for the sunrise, the sign of hope that begins each new day. During the night, we turn on our electric lights. During the vigil, we burn candles, especially the Easter candle, while praying the Office for the Dead. As the day fades into night, we find that we are accompanied in our waiting by Christ, the light of the world, the one who triumphed over death's darkness and walked into eternal light.

Lights help us to feel secure. Otherwise, we wouldn't have so many lining the streets of our cities or dusk-to-dawn fixtures in our yards or dark-sensitive night lights in the hallways and bathrooms of our homes. We enter into the darkness waiting, trusting, secure in our faith that God, who conquered death's darkness for Jesus with the light of resurrection, will do the same for the dead child and for us. Our faith in the resurrection should be as sure as the sunrise which scatters the darkness of night and spreads light throughout our day. After a night of rest, during which we wait for the morning, we rise from darkness into light.

Questions for Reflection: What experiences have you had of waiting in the darkness (such as illness, surgery, accident) for light (healing, success, solution)? How did your faith help you to keep watch?

Prayer: God of hope, out of the depths of my being I cry to you for help. Be with me in my waiting. Scatter my darkness with your light. When I face the death of a loved one, strengthen my hope in the resurrection of your Son, Jesus. You did not abandon him to the darkness of his tomb, but you raised him to the brilliant light of eternal life. He lives and reigns with you and the Holy Spirit, one God, for ever and ever. Amen.

Journal: Besides the cross, what do you consider to be other signs of your faith (such as a crucifix, an icon, a Bible)? Make a list and for each identify how it expresses your faith and hope in the resurrection of Christ.

CANTICLE: MEMORIES

Scripture: (Phil 2:6-11) Let the same mind be in you that was in Christ Jesus,

> [who was] born in human likeness
> and . . . found in human form. . . .
> . . . .
> . . . [A]t the name of Jesus
> every knee should bend,
> in heaven and on earth and under the earth,
> and every tongue should confess that
> Jesus Christ is Lord,
> to the glory of God the Father (2:5, 7bc, 10-11).

Order of Christian Funerals: par. 366.

Reflection: Over the years, we collect lots of knick-knacks, trinkets, and other types of mementos. One of my treasures consists of a small bottle of North Slope crude oil from Alaska; it reminds me of the three months I spent in the forty-ninth state on sabbatical several years ago. Another item filled with memories is a reproduction of a pottery oil lamp from Lyon, France; it reminds me of the Roman excavations I saw there, the fact that Gaul was once part of the Roman Empire, and other places I visited during that trip. When we look around our homes, we discover photo albums, Christmas ornaments, and candles that trigger memories of where we have travelled, places we have seen, people we have loved.

Before the end of the Office for the Dead, a family or a friend may speak in remembrance of the deceased infant, child, or teen. One way that this might be done is to use an object that brings to mind the memory of the dead. For an infant, the white garment and candle from baptism might be used if the baby was baptized. If the infant was not baptized, then the blanket in which the baby was wrapped or the footprint made on the birth certificate or a medal or something else given to the child might be used.

Memories might be sparked by a child's favorite toy, a Children's Bible, or, depending on the age of the child, something made in Sunday school or religion class. A teen's favorite compact disk; a Christian item, such as a statue, icon, or plaque; a banner, poster, or Bible or other book can be the catalyst for memories of the dead.

The purpose of someone speaking in remembrance of the dead is to help us work through some of our grief. By calling to mind the memories we have of the person and sharing those memories, we are able to mourn our loss and come to terms with the reality of death.

Just like we have mementos of the dead, we have memories of Jesus, too. His birth in human form is called to mind every year at Christmas when we display the creche with the child on the straw in the animal's feeding trough. We have the memory of his death in the form of a cross in our churches, on the walls of our homes, and maybe in our cars. We acknowledge Christ's presence in the eucharistic bread by our genuflection toward the tabernacle when we enter the chapel of reservation. When we say we believe that God's Son became a human being in the profession of faith, we bend our knee on March 25 (Annunciation of the Lord) and December 25 (Birth of the Lord) to remember that God's Son became one of us.

Our mementos of Jesus help us to declare that he is the Lord; they help us to remember what God did for us through Jesus' birth and death. As we remember all the dead, especially the dead infant, child, or teen, we praise God for giving them a share in the eternal life God gave to Jesus.

Questions for Reflection: What item in your home do you think best represents you? What memories do you hope it will trigger for others during your funeral rites? Have you included it in your funeral arrangements?

Prayer: God of heaven and earth, with my mind, heart, and lips I confess that your Son, Jesus Christ, is Lord to your honor and glory. Fill me with awe as I remember the miracle of his birth. Fill me with thanksgiving as I remember his death on the cross. And fill me with hope as I remember his resurrection from the dead. Grant this through Jesus Christ, who lives and reigns with you and the Holy Spirit, one God, for ever and ever. Amen.

Journal: Walk through your home and gather three to five mementos of people who have died. For each item indicate of whom it reminds you. Compose a short prayer of praise to God for each person, expressing your hope that each now shares eternal life.

READING: VICTORY THROUGH CHRIST

Scripture: (1 Cor 15:55-57) . . . [T]hanks be to God, who gives us the victory through our Lord Jesus Christ (15:57).

Order of Christian Funerals: par. 361.

Reflection: When we speak about winning a victory, it usually is in reference to winning at sports, achieving a position, or conquering an enemy. In a religious sense, however, Christ is the victor over death. Using the battle metaphor, Paul tells the Corinthians that Jesus entered into a war with death and beat the enemy. God raised Jesus to new life and made him victorious. Through Christ's resurrection, we share in eternal life.

God, who created people in God's own image and likeness, could not let death win and take people out of existence. As creatures, our unique reflection of the image of God would be lost for ever if death won the battle. Every human person is a single icon of the infinite facets of God's creativity. And, as such, no one can be lost. Otherwise, God would lose some of God's own reflection.

Through Christ's death and resurrection, God gave us the victory over death, awakening us to the nobility of the One whose image we are and promising that we would see God face to face. Since God is pure spirit, all of us, even the youngest, must pass through death to let go of everything that isn't pure spirit in order to enter into eternal life with God. Death enables us to live as the Spirit lives and to see God as God sees.

Silence following the reading of Scripture during the Office for the Dead provides time for the beauty of this message to sink in. The brief homily which follows the silence should help us to understand it better. We no longer fear death, since it has been conquered. Like the legendary phoenix, who rises reborn from its own ashes, what looks like death is really the leaving behind of what is no longer needed—a body—to share in the victory won by Jesus Christ.

No matter at what age we die—infant, child, teen, young or old adult, God has promised that we will not lose life through death, but achieve it eternally. God's life is traced in us by God. Because we are created in God's image, we die in security knowing that God loses no one, for all mirror who God is.

Questions for Reflection: What aspects of God do you image for others? In other words, what do you (who are created in God's image) reveal about God to other people? For each aspect identify how you hope others see God.

Prayer: Victorious God, by raising Jesus from the grave, you destroyed death and restored life to all your people. By giving your Son the victory over death, you have made it possible for me to share in your eternal life. With your Holy Spirit guide me in being who you created me to be. Help me to be the living image of Jesus Christ, who lives and reigns with you and the Holy Spirit, one God, for ever and ever. Amen.

Journal: Why do you think people die? Make a list of your reasons. Considering how death has been beaten by the victory of Christ's resurrection, how are your fears of death lessened?

CANTICLE OF MARY: GREAT THINGS

Scripture: (Luke 1:46-55) . . . Mary said,

> "My soul magnifies the Lord,
> and my spirit rejoices in God my Savior,
>
> . . . .
>
> for the Mighty One has done great things for me,
> and holy is his name" (1:46-47, 49).

Order of Christian Funerals: pars. 362, 363.

Reflection: Because we are limited in our perspective, we do not often see the great things God does for us until we reach our older years and begin approaching the inevitability of death. Our inability to see clearly, as God does, can cause much discomfort for friends and family during the funeral rites for an infant, a child, or a teen. One thing to remember is that God does great things in everyone's life—no matter how old a person may have been.

For example, conception, the union of one human egg and one human sperm out of trillions of possibilities is a great deed of God. One human being is conceived through the joining of two cells each carrying one-half of the total human genetic code.

Our belief is a great deed of God, who enables us to express our faith in our own way. It is a gift, undeserved, unmerited, unearned. The way we express our trust in God—no matter how primitive—is not God's understanding of God as the Mighty One is. We cannot judge each other; all we can do is stand back in awe and praise God for the great gift we have received.

God does great deeds by directing our days and years. While direction comes quietly, God leads us to our vocation, career, partner for life, service in ministry. We don't live the lives we've planned; we adjust to what we have been called—and God is smart enough to do it subtly. Into each of us God plants ideas and talents, watering them with grace and watching them grow into what God wants of us.

For such great things as those we praise the Mighty One during the Office for the Dead, and we proclaim God's name to be holy. We honor the altar, the sign of Christ, the minister, and the congregation with incense while we sing Mary's canticle of praise. We become a fragrance pleasing to God and, in Paul's words, the "aroma of Christ to God among those who are being saved" (2 Cor 2:15).

The incense also reminds us that just as our lives are fragrant, so they are filled with God's great things, no matter how old we are. Likewise, death is the last great thing the Mighty One does for each of us. We pass through it to eternal life. Until that day, however, the fragrant incense of the living praises God for the new life given to the dead, those who have already experienced God's greatest deed— eternal life.

Questions for Reflection: What do you number among the great things that God has done in your life? How do you think your age influences your ability to see God's great deeds?

Prayer: Mighty One, holy be your name. From conception to death, you never cease to do great things for me. Make me overflow with love for you and your people. With the help of the Holy Spirit, guide my days and years in your service. Fill me with the hope that you will do for me what you did for Jesus, your Son, and raise me up from death to share in his life. He is Lord for ever and ever. Amen.

Journal: Choose a member of your family who has died and whom you remember well. What great things did God do in that person's life? In what ways can what you see in the family member's life help you to understand the great things God is doing in your life?

Planning Funeral Rites

Whenever possible, ministers should involve the family in planning the funeral rites: in the choice of texts and rites provided in the ritual, in the selection of music for the rites, and in the designation of liturgical ministers.

Planning of the funeral rites may take place during the visit of the pastor or other minister at some appropriate time after the death and before the vigil service. Ministers should explain to the family the meaning and significance of each of the funeral rites, especially the vigil, the funeral liturgy, and the rite of committal.

—*Order of Christian Funerals,* par. 17

2. Related Rites and Prayers

Prayers after Death

Invitation to Prayer (no. 104):   A   B

Reading (no. 105):

   A   B   C   or no. chosen from Part III _____

The Lord's Prayer (no. 106):   A   B

Concluding Prayers:

   For the deceased person: No. 107 or no. 398

   For the mourners: No. 107 or no. 399

Blessing (no. 108):   A   B

MINISTERS

Bishop/Priest/Deacon/Leader   _____

Reader _____

Gathering in the Presence of the Body

Sign of the Cross (no. 112)

Scripture Verse (no. 113):   A   B

Sprinkling with Holy Water (no. 114):   A   B   C

Psalm (no. 115):   A   B   or no. in Part III _____

The Lord's Prayer (no. 116):   A   B

Concluding Prayer (no. 117):

   A   B   or no. chosen from nos. 398–399 _____

Blessing (no. 118):   A   B

MINISTERS

Bishop/Priest/Deacon/Leader _____

Reader _____

Transfer of the Body to the Church or to the Place of Committal

Invitation (no. 121)

Scripture Verse (no. 122):   A   B

Litany (no. 123)

The Lord's Prayer (no. 124)

Concluding Prayer (no. 125):

   A   B   C   or no. chosen from nos. 398–399 _____

Invitation to the Procession (no. 126)

Procession to the Church or to the Place of Committal: No. 127

   or no. chosen from Part III, 16:

      Antiphons and Psalms _____

   or Song: _____

MINISTERS

Bishop/Priest/Deacon/Leader _____

Reader _____

Song Leader/Cantor _____

Musicians _____

Pall Bearers _____

7. Vigil for a Deceased Child

INTRODUCTORY RITES

Greeting (no. 248):   A   B   C   D

Sprinkling with Holy Water or Brief Address (no. 249):   A   B

[Placing of the Pall] (no. 250)

Entrance Procession (Song) (no. 251): _____

[Placing of Christian Symbols] (no. 252)

Invitation to Prayer (no. 253)

Opening Prayer (no. 254):

    A   B   C   or no. chosen from nos. 398–399 _____

LITURGY OF THE WORD

First Reading:

    No. 256 or no. chosen from Part III _____

Responsorial Psalm:

    No. 257 or no. chosen from Part III _____

Gospel: No. 258 or no. chosen from Part III _____

Homily (no. 259):

PRAYER OF INTERCESSION

Litany (no. 260)

The Lord's Prayer (no. 261):   A   B

Concluding Prayer (no. 262):

    A   B   or no. chosen from nos. 398–399 _____

CONCLUDING RITE

Blessing (no. 263):   A   B

MINISTERS

Bishop/Priest/Deacon/Leader _____

Reader _____

Homilist _____

Song Leader/Cantor _____

Musicians _____

Pall Bearers _____

Pall Placers _____

Servers/Assistants _____

Christian Symbol Placers _____

8. Funeral Mass

INTRODUCTORY RITES

Greeting (no. 277): A   B   C   D

Sprinkling with Holy Water or Brief Address (no. 278):   A   B

[Placing of the Pall] (no. 279)

Entrance Procession (Song) (no. 280): _____

[Placing of Christian Symbols] (no. 281)

Opening Prayer (no. 282):

   A   B   C   D   or no. chosen from no. 398 _____

LITURGY OF THE WORD

Readings

   Old Testament Reading:

      No. chosen from Part III _____

   Responsorial Psalm:

      No. chosen from Part III _____

   New Testament Reading:

      No. chosen from Part III _____

   Alleluia Verses and Verses Before the Gospel:

      No. chosen from Part III _____

   Gospel: No. chosen from Part III _____

Homily (no. 284)

General Intercessions (no. 285):

   A   B   or no. chosen from no. 401 _____

LITURGY OF THE EUCHARIST

Hymn During the Preparation of the Gifts: _____

Communion Hymn: _____

FINAL COMMENDATION

Invitation to Prayer (no. 289):

   A   B   C   or no. chosen from no. 402 _____

Silence (no. 290)

[Signs of Farewell] (no. 291)

Song of Farewell (no. 292) or Other Song _____

Prayer of Commendation (no. 293):

   A   B   or no. chosen from no. 404 _____

PROCESSION TO THE PLACE OF COMMITTAL

(No. 294):   A   B   C   D

MINISTERS

Bishop/Priest/Deacon/Leader _____

Readers _____

Homilis _____

Song Leader/Cantor _____

Musicians _____

Pall Bearers _____

Pall Placers _____

Servers/Assistants _____

Christian Symbol Placers _____

Eucharistic Ministers _____

Gift Bearers _____

9. Funeral Liturgy Outside Mass

INTRODUCTORY RITES

Greeting (no. 296):   A   B   C   D

Sprinkling with Holy Water or Brief Address (no. 297):   A   B

[Placing of the Pall] (no. 298)

Entrance Procession (Song) (no. 299): _____

[Placing of Christian Symbols] (no. 300)

Invitation to Prayer (no. 301)

Opening Prayer (no. 302):

    A   B   C   D   or no. chosen from nos. 398–399 _____

LITURGY OF THE WORD

Readings

    Old Testament Reading:

        No. chosen from Part III _____

    Responsorial Psalm:

        No. chosen from Part III _____

    New Testament Reading:

        No. chosen from Part III _____

    Alleluia Verses and Verses Before the Gospel:

        No. chosen from Part III _____

    Gospel: No. chosen from Part III _____

Homily (no. 304)

General Intercessions:

    No. 305 or no. chosen from no. 401 _____

The Lord's Prayer (no. 306):   A   B

FINAL COMMENDATION

Invitation to Prayer (no. 310):

    A   B   C   or no. chosen from no. 402 _____

Silence (no. 311)

[Signs of Farewell] (no. 312)

Song of Farewell (no. 313):

    A   B   or other song _____

Prayer of Commendation (no. 314):

   A   B   or no. chosen from no. 404 _____

PROCESSION TO THE PLACE OF COMMITTAL

(No. 315):   A   B   C   D

MINISTERS

Bishop/Priest/Deacon/Leader _____

Readers _____

Homilist _____

Song Leader/Cantor _____

Musicians _____

Pall Bearers _____

Pall Placers _____

Servers/Assistants _____

Christian Symbol Placers _____

10. Rite of Committal

Invitation (no. 319)

Scripture Verse (no. 320):   A   B   C   D

Prayer over the Place of Committal (no. 321):   A   B   C

   or no. chosen from no. 405 _____

Committal (no. 322):

   A   B   or no. chosen from no. 406 _____

Intercessions: No. 323 or no. chosen from no. 407 _____

The Lord's Prayer (no. 324)

Concluding Prayer (no. 325):

   A   B   C   or no. chosen from no. 408 _____

Prayer over the People (no. 326):   A   B

MINISTERS

Bishop/Priest/Deacon/Leader _____

Reader _____

Song Leader/Cantor _____

Musicians _____

Pall Bearers _____

Servers/Assistants _____

11. Rite of Committal with Final Commendation

Invitation (no. 327)

Scripture Verse (no. 328):   A   B   C   D

Prayer over the Place of Committal (no. 329):   A   B   C

   or no. chosen from no. 405 _____

Invitation to Prayer (no. 330):   A   B   C

   or no. chosen from no. 402 _____

Silence (no. 331)

[Signs of Farewell] (no. 332)

Song of Farewell (no. 333):   A   B   or other song: _____

Prayer of Commendation (no. 334):   A   B

   or no. chosen from no. 404 _____

Committal (no. 335)

Prayer over the People (no. 336):   A   B

MINISTERS

Bishop/Priest/Deacon/Leader _____

Reader _____

Song Leader/Cantor _____

Musicians _____

Pall Bearers _____

Servers/Assistants _____

12. Rite of Final Commendation for an Infant

Brief Address (no. 337)

Scripture Verse (no. 338):   A   B

Blessing of the Body (no. 339)

The Lord's Prayer (no. 340)

Prayer of Commendation (no. 341)

Blessing (no. 342):   A   B

MINISTERS

Bishop/Priest/Deacon/Leader   _____

Reader _____

Servers/Assistants _____

17. Morning Prayer

Introductory Verse (no. 374)

Hymn (no. 375): _____

Psalmody (no. 376):

First Psalm

Canticle

Second Psalm: A   B

Reading: No. 377 or no. chosen from Part III _____

Homily (no. 377)

Responsory (no. 378)

Canticle of Zechariah (no. 379)

Intercessions (no. 380)

The Lord's Prayer (no. 381)

Concluding Prayer (no. 382):

    A   B   C   or no. chosen from no. 398 _____

Dismissal (no. 383):   A   B

[Procession to the Place of Committal] (no. 384):   A   B   C   D

MINISTERS

Bishop/Priest/Deacon/Leader   _____

Reader   _____

Homilist _____

Song Leader/Cantor _____

Musicians _____

Pall Bearers _____

Servers/Assistants _____

18. Evening Prayer

Introductory Verse (no. 386)

Hymn (no. 387):   _____

Psalmody (no. 388):

   First Psalm

   Second Psalm

   Canticle

Reading: No. 389 or no. chosen from Part III _____

Homily (no. 389)

Responsory (no. 390):   A   B

Canticle of Mary (no. 391)

Intercessions (no. 392)

The Lord's Prayer (no. 393)

Concluding Prayer (no. 394):

   A   B   C   or no. chosen from no. 398 _____

Dismissal (no. 395):   A   B

MINISTERS

Bishop/Priest/Deacon/Leader _____

Reader _____

Homilist _____

Song Leader/Cantor _____

Musicians _____

Servers/Assistants _____

Annotated List of Scripture Texts

14. Funerals for Baptized Children

Psalms
23

> The Lord is my shepherd; there is nothing I shall want.

25

> O Lord, do not remember the failings of my youth.

42

> My soul is thirsting for the living God: when shall I see God face to face?

148

> Let everyone praise the name of the Lord.

Isaiah 25:6a, 7-9

> God will destroy death for ever.

Lamentations 3:22-26

> It is good to wait in silence for the saving help of God.

Matthew 11:25-30

> The things hidden from the learned and the clever have been revealed to children.

Mark 10:13-16

> We must accept the reign of God like a child.

John
6:37-40 or 6:37-39

> The will of the Father is that Jesus should lose nothing of what God has given to him.

6:51-58

On the last day, I will raise up all who eat my flesh and drink my blood.

11:32-38, 40

If you believe, you will see the glory of God.

19:25-30

Standing at the cross were Jesus' mother, Mary the wife of Clopas, and Mary of Magdala.

Romans
6:3-4, 8-9

If we die with Christ, we shall also live with him.

14:7-9

No matter whether we live or die, we belong to the Lord.

1 Corinthians 15:20-23

All people will be brought to life in Christ.

Ephesians 1:3-5

God chose us in Christ, before the creation of the world, to be holy.

1 Thessalonians 4:13-14, 18

God will raise those who have fallen asleep in Christ.

Revelation
7:9-10, 15-17

The Lamb will shepherd them, leading them to life-giving water and wiping away every tear from their eyes.

21:1a, 3-5a

There will be no more death, mourning, wailing, or pain.

15. Funerals for Children Who Died Before Baptism

Psalm 25
> To you, O Lord, I lift up my soul. You will rescue me.

Isaiah 25:6a, 7-8b
> God will destroy death forever and wipe away the tears from all faces.

Lamentations 3:22-26
> It is good to wait in silence for the saving help of the Lord.

Matthew 11:25-30
> What the Father has hidden from the learned and the clever, God has revealed to children.

Mark 15:33-46
> Jesus said, "My God, my God, why have you forsaken me?" and breathed his last.

John 19:25-30
> Here is your son. Here is your mother.

Index of Scripture Texts